CHALLENGING INVISIBILITY

CHALLENGING INVISIBILITY

Practices *of* Care
with Older Women

KAREN D. SCHEIB

CHALICE
P R E S S
ST. LOUIS, MISSOURI

Cover art: Getty Images
Cover and interior design: Elizabeth Wright

This book is printed on acid-free, recycled paper.

Visit Chalice Press on the World Wide Web at
www.chalicepress.com

10 9 8 7 6 5 4 3 2 1   04 05 06 07 08 09

Library of Congress Cataloging–in–Publication Data

Scheib, Karen D.
  Challenging invisibility : practices of care with older women / Karen D. Scheib.
    p. cm.
  Includes bibliographical references.
  ISBN 0-8272-0494-9 (pbk. : alk. paper)
  1. Church work with older women. I. Title.
  BV4435.3.S34 2004
  259'.3'082–dc22
                                                                    2004002459

Printed in the United States of America

Contents

*This book is dedicated to
the memory of my mother,
Ann Keaty Scheib,
and my grandmother
Katherine Scheib*

Preface

Older women have long been a part of my world. When I was a child, there were few children on my block and I could often be found at Mrs. Johnson's house down the street. After Dr. Johnson fooled me with his trick ink spill, for which I fell every time, Mrs. Johnson usually filled me with milk, cookies, and stories. As I began college, my grandmother came to live with us to help care for my mother and was my first college "roommate." I loved to hear the stories of how she met my grandfather dancing, also a favorite pastime of mine. When I was an adult, I would ask her for romantic advice and hear tales of her courtship.

When I first began my ministry in 1980, I was a young woman of twenty-five. Reflecting on how members of my congregations shaped my emerging identity as a minister, I realized that many of these were older women who served as mentors and guides to me. Addie Smith was not only the treasurer who helped me to understand the world of church finance; she also taught me to crochet a baby blanket for my nephew. As a relatively new pastor, I believed it was my job to minister to everyone else, but I soon realized that these women had much to teach me about the Christian faith, ministry, and what it meant to be a church. After all, they'd been Christians and members of their congregations longer than the span of my life.

When I began doctoral studies, I did not encounter much literature in the field that addressed the lives of older women, nor was the more general topic of aging explored. Yet the majority of my pastoral care ministry in the church continued to be with older women, who often formed the bulk of the membership. This disjunction between the realities in the church and the academy was not immediately apparent to me. Only recently have I wondered why older women, so present in the church, were absent in the literature of pastoral care and counseling and in my teaching.

This disjunction between the significant presence of older women in the church and their relative invisibility in pastoral care literature and seminary curriculum is the primary motivation for this book. In the pages ahead I argue that women's invisibility is socially constructed, and I propose a model of care expressed through a set of practices that challenge this invisibility. I write as one whose life has been significantly influenced by older women and as their advocate. This work is directed primarily to pastors, seminary students, the church, and other communities and individuals who yearn for a theologically grounded approach to working with and caring for older women.

Although a book of this sort might appear to be a solitary endeavor, it is not. It would have been impossible without the fifteen women who shared their life stories through the interview process. I extend my sincere gratitude to them and to the many women whom I engaged in informal conversation. All were willing to tell me things no one thinks to tell you as you grow older. I am also grateful for the older women in the congregations I served, who modeled vibrant aging and embodied narratives of resistance to the cultural definitions of age.

The technical matters of bringing a book such as this to fruition include the research project itself and much else. Katherine L. Davis, who conducted and videotaped a number of the interviews and assisted in the initial analysis of the data, most ably assisted me in the interview research. This project would not have been possible without her help. I also want to express my thanks to a number of able office assistants, including Saralyn Massenlink, Richard Fuss, Denise Morgan, and Michael Waide, who willingly fetched books, searched the Web, repaired footnotes, and performed a variety of other tasks.

Scholarship emerges in the midst of a community of teaching and learning. The support of Candler School of Theology, through a research grant that funded the interview project and a leave that allowed completion of the manuscript, are much appreciated. Colleagues at Candler School of Theology, Emory University, challenged me through stimulating conversations, read portions of the manuscript, pointed me to resources, and provided general encouragement. My thanks to Nancy Eiesland, Liz Bounds, Rodney Hunter, Joy McDougal, E. Brooks Holifield, and Mary Elizabeth Molino Moore for these various expressions of support. I am indebted to my friend and colleague Roberta Bondi for her mentoring and unflagging companionship as this book came to life. My longtime friend Anne Carey provided encouragement, a sympathetic ear, and a discerning eye. Although authors often have good ideas, they have to take shape and form. I am most grateful to Ulrike Guthrie for her editorial assistance and for coaxing fine words from a reluctant pen.

A word of thanks also goes to Jon Berquist for his support of this project from the beginning.

Finally, I extend my deepest gratitude to my husband, Jonathan Spingarn, whose practices of care included listening, cooking, encouraging, and weathering the varying moods of a working author, all with tender good humor. For this extended community of support I give thanks.

CHAPTER 1

Invisible Women

"Old women are invisible. Didn't you know that? We are invisible." Ann, seventy, a retired social worker, was replying to my question, "How do you feel older women are perceived?" Her response surprised me because she is quite active in her community. She is a middle school mentor, takes an active role in local politics, and volunteers in her congregation. Still, she feels invisible, especially to younger people. Ann comments further: "Really. I mean, if I walk down the street in any town, most people—men and women, up to I'd say the age of fifty-five to sixty—don't notice me. I am invisible."

Ann is not alone in her experience. Dorothy, an active seventy-two-year-old woman and a fine artist, has also felt invisible as an older woman. She was in the middle of building a new home and studio in the country when I sat down to ask her about her experience of aging. She responded by relating a recent incident that occurred while volunteering in her grandson's third grade classroom. As she went about her assigned classroom tasks, the younger mothers interacted with her minimally, talking mostly to each other. She found this experience quite disconcerting. She says, "As you get older you cease to exist in the eyes of some younger people; you become invisible. No one seems interested in who you are or what you do. It is disconcerting."

Such experiences of invisibility occur in the church and in the larger culture. Rose, a petite and energetic woman of seventy, has been active in the church all her life as both a lay member and minister's wife. She is not unaware of her age, yet aging is not the primary category through which Rose usually interprets her experience. Reminders of her age often come from her interactions with younger persons, such as this incident, which struck her as "really strange."

Rose was volunteering at a church event preparing for a luncheon. At the buffet line, she found herself standing next to two young women who talked with each other about their positive experiences with older women, yet ignored Rose, working right beside them. She describes her experience:

> They were having this conversation about how they really enjoyed knowing some of the older women [in the church]. I was standing right there and they had never spoken to me, and never did. It was just as odd as it could be…I'd say they were in their late thirties to early forties. It was strange. That was really startling to me. I had not thought about being invisible to that point. But since then I have realized that older women don't attract the attention that younger women do. Older women are really sort of past noticing somehow.

Rose suggests that her invisibility is due in part to stereotypical images of older women that shape these younger women's perceptions of her. She refers to this as the little old lady syndrome, and says, "Little old ladies just really don't seem to count for much to a lot of people."

Jane's experience of invisibility in the church began with a move at age ninety to an assisted living facility. At the same time she decided to give up her driver's license. As a result, she no longer can attend the congregation to which she has belonged for some time. Staying connected to the church is important to her, and her commitment is evident in the arrangements she has made to have her pledge automatically deducted from her checking account monthly and deposited in the church's account. She has not forgotten the church, but she feels as if it has forgotten her. Jane was widowed twice and has lost both her children, and the support of the church community is quite important to her. She has received only two visits from the church in the past year. This invisibility has distressed her.

> Well, I have gotten depressed about that a few times. I told my minister one time when he came here. They don't come much, just once in a while. The first time he came I said, "You know, I sure am glad you came because I had just about decided that with our church it was out of sight out of mind." I told him that. I felt like as long as I was there everything was fine, but when you are not there, you are forgotten.

This invisibility felt by older women contrasts sharply with demographic realities. Older women currently outnumber older men in the United States, and the proportion increases with age. In 2001 the U.S. Administration on Aging reported that women make up 58 percent of the population over the age of sixty and 70 percent of the population over age eighty-five. Demographic trends indicate that this older population will double between 1999 and 2030. By 2030 older adults will constitute about 20 percent of the population, and the majority of this group will be women.[1]

Constructing Invisibility

How do older women become an invisible majority? Clearly it is not because they are few in number. I have come to believe that invisibility results from social, political, and economic factors that provide the context in which older women age.[2] This social context is not neutral toward aging, but defines or constructs what it means to grow and to be old. Understanding aging as largely socially constructed means that our definition of old age is not universal or fixed.[3] For example, the concept of an "old woman" is not just a descriptive term, but reflects cultural beliefs that can change over time.[4] We may not be conscious of these beliefs and attitudes, but they become visible in our social institutions and practices.

This social construction of age has particular consequences for women.[5] Because our current cultural beliefs about "old women" are generally negative, elderly women have little status in the culture. We seldom see them as attractive or perceive them as able to make significant contributions to society. Such attitudes do not reflect a natural outcome of the aging process, but result from the dominant cultural ideology of aging.

The church exists within the larger culture and thus is not immune from the cultural construction of age that results in negative images of older women. Although in some congregations the contributions of older women are recognized and honored, in many others older women are pushed to the sidelines and become an invisible majority in the church.[6] Rose's and Jane's experiences of invisibility occurred in the church. How sad that this happens so much in the church, a community that claims that human beings–of all ages–reflect the image of God and hence deserve attention. As a community that seeks to embody redemption, the church is called to challenge the invisibility of older women and its contribution to that invisibility.

A Call to the Church

Why should the church be concerned with older women, and why focus on women rather than all older adults? First, older women will increasingly be represented in many congregations as the whole of society ages. Some of these congregations will consist largely of older women. If negative attitudes persist, these churches will be seen as dying or problem churches, and both the worth of these women and their resources for ministry will be lost. More important, the very identity of the church as a redemptive community is at stake here.

An older woman is generally defined in the gerontological literature as a woman over the age of sixty. In the United States our current definitions of "old age" are closely tied to retirement ages as established in the Social Security legislation of 1935. This definition of "old" is related to productive labor rather than to abilities or life experiences and is accepted in both the larger culture and academic literature. The consequences of this definition will be addressed in later chapters. Because the life expectancy of older adults has increased considerably, and with it often the physical and mental acuity of older adults, old age may cover a span of thirty years or more. Gerontologists now distinguish between the young old, ages sixty to seventy-five; the middle old, seventy-five to eighty-five; and the oldest old, eighty-five and older.[7] Older women are not a homogeneous group, but embrace a host of ages, ethnicities, socioeconomic classes, educational levels, and varying states of health.

Why focus on older women? First, the majority of older adults *are* women. Older women outnumber men in the United States, and "the proportion of the population that is female increases with age."[8] In 2001 women accounted for a majority of the population aged sixty-five and older. In 1999 there were 20.2 million older women (over 65) and 14.3 million older men, or a ratio of 141 women for every 100 men. The sex ratio increased with age, ranging from 118/100 for the sixty-five to sixty-nine age group to a high of 237/100 for persons eighty-five and over.[9] Demographic trends indicate that the older population will continue to grow in the next two to three decades. If the sex ratios continue to be similar to today's trends, this means a very large population of older women.

Second, older women have received less attention in scholarly studies on aging. One might expect that gerontologists aware of the sexual demographics of aging would have given special attention to the issues of women's aging. Although this is now the case, it is a relatively recent development. Early gerontological studies did not distinguish between women's and men's experiences of aging. Feminist pastoral theologians paid little attention to women's experience of aging until the 1990s. Until the late 1980s, older women were also overlooked in women's studies.[10]

The third reason for focusing on older women is that aging itself is a gendered experience, meaning that as they age, women "disappear" from view in different ways and for reasons different from those for older men. Some of these reasons are the consequence of the unique interaction of ageism and sexism. An example of this gendered invisibility is evident in the few older women occupying prominent positions of public leadership in the United States, in contrast to the number of older men in such positions. Older women are less often depicted in media than are older men, including magazine advertisements, television, and feature films.

Understanding the construction of older women's invisibility in both church and society requires a perspective that moves beyond the individual experiences of aging to an analysis of the social forces that shape the experience of aging in America. However, much of the current literature on aging in gerontology, as well as pastoral care, emphasizes the personal (primarily biological and psychological) dimensions of aging.[11] In the pastoral care literature this emphasis is reflected in a concern with spiritual well-being, aging as time of personal spiritual growth, and personal adjustment to the problems of aging through pastoral counseling.[12] Although this individual approach to aging is valid and needed, it can overlook the social context that impacts one's experience of aging.

What is needed is a pastoral approach to aging that takes into account the social context to complement the individualistic approach. Developing such an approach requires not only sociological analysis but also theological reflection. But how do our theological claims actively challenge cultural constructions of age that render older women invisible? How might such a revisioning of older women reshape our ministry with them? Holding our theological beliefs together with awareness of the social construction of age allows us to critique our beliefs and practices toward older women in our congregations. This process of critical reflection can help us envision Christian communities that can be good places to grow old.

To empower congregations to be such good places, we must think about both the meaning of aging and the nature of church communities. An analysis of the social construction of aging can help us understand how meanings of aging change, while reclaiming aging as a part of human experience. Thinking about the nature of church communities requires us to develop an ecclesiology that embraces persons as they age. The church is called to be not only an inclusive community but a redemptive and prophetic community that opposes the marginalization of older women.

Constructing a Model of Care

I propose a model of care and a set of practices to challenge women's invisibility and assist congregations in being good places to grow old. Although I draw on the insights of gerontology, sociology, psychology, and anthropology, I am writing as a practical and pastoral theologian. Our cultural inability to see older women clearly and to respond effectively to the issues they face is not simply a social or political problem, or even a problem of effective ministerial technique. Responses formulated only from these perspectives will be inadequate. I am convinced that the cultural invisibility of older women is also a theological problem that requires a theological response. Developing such a response requires several steps. First, we must identify the basic assumptions and principles informing our work, which includes beginning with women's experiences. Clarifying the method through which various theories are integrated is the second step. The third step is naming the specific theological and social science theories informing the work. The fourth step is identifying the particular context in which this model is most appropriate. Finally, we describe particular practices embodying the model.

Hearing Women's Voices

To move toward developing a model of care, we begin with women's experiences of invisibility. By hearing older women themselves tell their stories, explain their perceptions, and share their feelings, we become aware of the powerful effects of the social construction of aging on a woman's sense of self as she ages. In order to hear the voices of older women, I conducted a qualitative study, using an ethnographic interview methodology in which I invited older women to tell their stories and reflect on their experiences of aging.

Description of the Study

I conducted a small qualitative interview study in order to enter the life-worlds of older women. My research assistant and I interviewed fifteen women age sixty-five or older in open-ended interviews of sixty to ninety minutes each. Each woman was interviewed one time, with the exception of one participant, who requested two follow-up conversations, based on additional insights she had following the first interview. I used an ethnographic interviewing technique and invited the women to begin by telling their stories. Follow-up questions sought to evoke the woman's sense of herself and her experience of herself as she aged by comparing life experiences at different points across the life span. Each participant was asked questions about others' perception of her and her perception of what makes someone "old." We also asked about the challenges and opportunities of her stage in life. A final question asked what advice the participant would give to young pastors working with older women.

Because this was a qualitative study designed to enter the life-world of a few older women, I did not seek a representative sample. Participants were recruited in one of two ways: through advertisements at a senior housing complex and through referral. All participants are Protestant Christians, and most are members of old-line congregations. All the women are currently involved in a local congregation or have been involved at some point in their lives. Three of the participants were African American women, and two participants were lesbian women. The youngest woman was sixty-five; the oldest was ninety-one. Most participants were in their seventies or eighties. The majority of the women were middle class, but at least three had incomes at or below the poverty line.[13]

Discoveries from the Study

Through the interviews I quickly discovered that being identified as an "old woman" can come as a surprise. I also learned that age is not the primary category that these women use to describe themselves or their lives. These women are or were wives, mothers, sisters, teachers, clerks, learners, explorers, and many other things. These women were aware of their aging, but it was not their primary self-identification.

Conducting these interviews alerted me to my own preconceived notions about aging. At the beginning of this project I also assumed that the term *older woman* was neutral, merely descriptive of a stage in life. What I discovered is that this is true only if you are younger and describing someone else. *Old* is not a neutral term in U.S. culture and is not merely a marker of chronology or time passed. To the women interviewed, being old meant fragility, senility, being used up, without purpose, or obsolete. At the same time that the women articulated these definitions of old, most of them did not identity themselves as old.

I also thought it would be easy for older women to discuss their experiences of aging. I quickly found that this was not the case, since aging is not a category most of us use to organize life experience. This discovery led to a change in the interview questions.

The interviews also reinforced the importance of recognizing the unique experience of each human being. As I listened to the women's stories, it was clear that each individual life was embedded in a web of relationships and connections. A woman's story was never solely about herself, but always included the important people in her life. These insights alerted me to the need to articulate the basic assumptions informing my approach to care, which includes attention to the dynamic interplay between individuality and connection.

Basic Assumptions and Principles

Enabling congregations to be good places to grow old requires us to challenge individualistic assumptions influencing our thinking about both aging and the church.

A basic assumption undergirding the proposed model of care is that human beings are not primarily autonomous but are essentially relational and communal. Our identity as individuals is not formed in isolation or by purely internal psychological factors, nor are we shaped simply by the pressures of social forces. Identity is the result of a complex interaction of factors and emerges from the matrix of interpersonal, communal, and social relationships.

This basic understanding of human experience leads to five assumptions that shape a model of care. First, the assertion of the centrality of relationality and community affirms that human beings are created in and for communion with God and the rest of creation. Second, the church, or ecclesial community, is formed by divine initiative as an expression of God's desire for communion. Such a community should be constituted by love, acceptance, forgiveness, commitment, and intimacy.[14] Life within the community is marked by mutuality and reciprocity. Mutuality does not imply that everyone has equal and identical roles in a community, but rather that all share power and responsibility for communal life. Prophetic witness in the larger world expresses the distinctive nature of ecclesial communities. Third, because humans are essentially relational, psychological development is understood as a relational process occurring within a social context. The meanings of concepts such as self and personhood are viewed as socially constructed. Personality theories highlighting psychological development as an interpersonal rather than intrapsychic process inform this model. Fourth, the social context is not neutral. A critical assessment of the process that constructs the social context is required. This assessment includes attention to dynamics of power in the construction of social reality. Fifth, this critical assessment of social milieu fosters the valuing of contextuality, individual differences, and cultural diversity. Diversity and unity are not seen as mutually exclusive; each is an integral part of complex human communities. The basis of unity is the shared narrative of the Christian tradition, which is expressed through differing cultural traditions and in a variety of contexts.

These five assumptions define a model of pastoral and congregational care that is theologically informed, takes into account the social context, attends to clinical insights that illumine the particularities of individual lives, and is expressed through specific ecclesial practices.

Pastoral Theological Method

With these basic assumptions in place, the second step toward building the model of care is to identify methodology. Beginning with older women's experiences of invisibility represents feminist methodological commitment. Feminist pastoral methodologies explore women's experiences of exclusion, such as invisibility, that occur as a result of gender discrimination over the life span.[15] From this perspective, invisibility is problematic and is not seen as a normal consequence of aging. Experience as a beginning point of reflection is also a characteristic of the revised correlational approach, which I also employ. A critical correlational method connects insights from experience, contemporary culture, and social science with insights from the Christian tradition in order to understand and challenge this invisibility.[16]

One of the questions posed by a critical correlational approach is the relation between theological and social science theory. Does one take precedence over the other? This question can be resolved by understanding that social science theories and theology approach questions from different starting points. Theology begins with metaphorical or visional claims about the nature of the created order, whereas social science theories generally begin with description of human interaction. Implicit in any theology are assumptions about how the metaphors of human life are actually lived out, whereas embedded in any social science theory are metaphors about the world.[17]

The methodological commitment to begin with women's experience shaped my choice of research method. Because my goal was to privilege women's voices, I chose a qualitative method and followed the guidelines for ethnographic interviewing.[18] Much of the literature in gerontology employs quantitative research methods focusing on measurable variables and large representative samples. It may be easier to generalize from such studies, but they usually focus on a narrow, externally measurable dimension of experience. Qualitative studies provide a glimpse into a life-world, but the conclusions one can draw are limited. I have tried to address these limitations by bringing the insights from my study into dialogue with other empirical studies on women's experiences of aging.

Theoretical Perspectives

Identifying the method employed to bring various theoretical perspectives together becomes meaningless if we don't also clearly identify the perspectives informing the construction of the model of care. In the method discussed earlier, the theological metaphor of relationality and community as central to human life operates as a guiding metaphor for a model of care and acts as a criterion for the selection of informing theological and social science theories.[19]

Theology

The theological perspective for a model of care that enables Christian communities to be good places to grow old draws significantly on recent work in Trinitarian theology. Addressing the issues of older women in dialogue from this perspective continues the development of a pastoral doctrine of the Trinity, which draws primarily on theological anthropology and ecclesiology.[20] Theological anthropology helps us think about aging as a part of human experience. For these reflections I rely on the work on theology of aging by K. Brynolf Lyon.[21] I supplement Lyon's view by drawing on Alistair McFayden's Trinitarian anthropology, which views personhood as relational.[22]

My primary focus here is on issues of ecclesiology, because previous work in the theology of aging provides an adequate articulation of aging as a dimension of human experience.[23] The nature of a church community that is a good place to grow old, however, has received less attention. Thus my task is to attend to the ecclesiological theories and practices that encourage such communities. Informing my reflections on ecclesiology is recent work in communion ecclesiology, represented by Elizabeth Johnson and Miroslav Volf, who both articulate visions of Christian community reflecting recent Trinitarian thought.[24] Any ecclesiology, of course, has its own implicit anthropological assumptions, which must be named.

Social Science

Whereas theology helps us explore the nature of communities in which we might grow old, social science theories help us to describe various dimensions of aging. One of the challenges in using social science research, however, is that this research is informed by multiple and competing theories of aging and so one must identify the theoretical perspectives one is using.[25] Theories of aging can be distinguished in two primary ways. The first distinction explored here is between theories that look primarily at social forces that affect aging (macro-level theories) and those that focus on experience of aging in individual lives (micro-level theories). The second distinction examined is between normative and interpretive theories. Normative perspectives often follow the methodologies of the natural sciences, assume that facts of aging are waiting to be discovered and described, and look for universal explanations of behavior.[26] The interpretive perspective holds that people "construct and make use of norms" but that these norms are not universal, nor do people necessarily adhere to such norms.[27] The social scientist working from the interpretive perspective defines her role as understanding social behavior.

Critical gerontology, the perspective I use in this work, seeks to link macro- and micro-levels of analysis and is interpretive rather than normative.[28] A critical theory of aging helps define the problems associated with aging as more than a personal issue. Proponents of critical theory explore the social construction of age and the ways in which personal meanings of aging are shaped by social definitions mediated through institutions and cultural practices. From this perspective, race, class, and gender are also socially constructed realities that intersect with age to influence a particular individual's experience. For example, Carroll Estes, a proponent of critical gerontology, develops a specific political economy theory of aging and argues that many of the problems facing the elderly in the United States are largely a consequence of the social construction of age.[29] Critical gerontology is especially helpful in exploring how social practices and public policy shape the meanings of aging.

An older woman's identity is influenced by the larger social construction of aging. Robert Atchley's continuity theory provides an explanation for the way in which these larger constructions of aging are internalized or rejected. Continuity theory argues that people seek to maintain a continuous sense of self.[30] Many older women experience a conflict between their own internal sense of self and socially constructed perceptions of old women. Continuity theory and critical gerontology allow us to examine further the interaction between the social context and personal experiences of aging.

Context

The social construction of aging that renders older women invisible occurs both within the larger society and in Christian communities and congregations. This book focuses primarily on the context of Christian congregations. Because Christian congregations are diverse and reflect differing denomination, ethnic, and theological perspectives, I have limited my study to congregations within the old-line Protestant denominations.[31] The model of care I propose is most appropriate for this context, though it may also have relevance in other settings.

This choice of focus on old-line Protestantism is for two primary reasons. First, because these congregations are often made up of individuals representing the dominant cultural group, primarily persons of European American heritage, they are often less aware of the way in which dominant cultural attitudes impinge on religious practices. For example, ageism may be accepted as a cultural value, and practices that resist dominant cultural norms may be less evident in mainline congregations. Thus I believe invisibility presents a particular problem for older women in these congregations.

Second, although the problem of invisibility affects women of all races and ethnic backgrounds, women of color often experience the invisibility of age as compounding their lifelong experience of invisibility due to the interaction of race and gender discrimination. Racism, not ageism, may be perceived as a more pressing constraint. In addition, congregational practices of honoring elders often provides a counterbalance to the dominant cultural attitudes and practices in some ethnic congregations, including many African American and Asian American communities.[32] In addition to these primary factors, two secondary considerations served to limit my reflections to a particular context. The first of these is that the majority of my interview subjects, including one of the three African American women, attend or attended old-line churches, and the second is that this is the primary context in which I have lived out my vocation as a pastoral caregiver. Not only do I know this context but because I stand within it, I feel I can speak a word of challenge to it.

Ecclesial Practices

The model of care developed here becomes embodied through particular ecclesial practices. *Relational practices* support and tend to the interpersonal relationships and communities that nurture older women. *Narrative practices* enable us to tell different stories about what it means to age and what it means to be an older woman, thus reshaping our images of aging. Through *prophetic practices* of pastoral intervention and public policy we become advocates for older women. Enabling churches to be good places to grow old means developing these practices where needed and strengthening them where they occur sporadically and unconsciously in the life of the church. These practices, described in more detail in chapter 3, are explored in the remaining chapters through the stories emerging from the interviews.

Organization of the Book

Here I have suggested that older women fade from view as a consequence of the cultural construction of age. In chapter 2 I explore how this invisibility is constructed. Using the tools of critical gerontology, I examine processes such as cultural imperialism and binary thinking, through which certain images of aging become dominant. Following a basic introduction to the constructionist approach, I examine the history of aging as an example of how images of aging reflect cultural ideals. Two contemporary approaches to aging, the biomedical model and popular cultural images, are critiqued.

The ways in which these contemporary approaches to age shape practices of care in congregations is the starting point for chapter 3. This chapter seeks to develop a theologically grounded model of aging, rooted in a particular vision of the church, which challenges the invisibility of older women. I propose a model of the church as a community of gracious inclusion, which embodies this vision through three practices of care. Narrative practices are foundational and provide the means for articulating an alternative construction of aging. Relational practices include tending relationships and creating communities of support. Through prophetic practices of care we seek to challenge beliefs and practices that diminish older women. These practices include being advocates for older women, especially concerning economic security, abuse, and caregiving, three issues that can negatively affect the lives of older women.

Practices of care are explored in more detail in chapters 4 through 7. Chapter 4 focuses on narrative practices and details various forms of narratives. Three stories emerging from the interviews illustrate practices of addressing conflicting narratives. Chapters 5 and 6 examine relational practices of care in the lives of single, married, and partnered women and discuss family relationships such as the mother-child bond, as well as the role played by older women's friendships. Chapter 7 sets forth prophetic practices of care such as advocacy, affirming narratives of resistance, and juxtaposing the Christian story with cultural narratives of aging.

The Women of This Book

You will meet eleven of the fifteen women interviewed and will enter into their lives through their words. Through their stories we will explore practices of care that might challenge older women's invisibility.[33] Although using the last names of older women is often a sign of respect, I have chosen to use first names (all pseudonyms) in order to create familiarity and intimacy; most of the women interviewed asked to be addressed by their first names.

Joan is an eighty-three-year-old European American woman, recently widowed at the time of the study. She lives on her own in an independent living apartment in a senior housing complex. She took on the role of caregiver for her husband preceding his death.

Julie, eighty-two, is a European American woman living in the same complex as Joan. Julie faced significant economic challenges following the death of her second husband. She credits the ongoing support of her church for helping her make it through a difficult time.

Katherine is sixty-six, of African American descent, and lives in a townhouse in the community. A retired schoolteacher who is divorced, she moved to the area to be closer to her children and grandchildren. She is committed to bridging differences.

Sarah is seventy-three, of European American descent, and is also a retired teacher. She lives with her husband in their home in the suburbs. Following a difficult transition to retirement, Sarah went back to work part-time.

Elizabeth is a sixty-five-year-old woman who lives with her partner **Ann,** age seventy. Both women, who are of European American descent, are retired and have moved to what was their country home as their permanent residence.

Mary, eighty-four, a European American woman, was the only newlywed in my study. She lives at the same residence as Joan and Julie, where she met her second husband several months before. She had been married about four months at the time of the interview.

Rose, seventy, also of European American heritage and a retired teacher, is discovering a new life freed from the role of preacher's wife following her husband's retirement. Although she enjoyed the role at the time, she is discovering it was more constricting than she realized.

Kate is single, European American, seventy-two, and also visually impaired. She is discovering new freedoms and challenges following the death of her mother, for whom she was caretaker the last few years of her life, before her mother's death at age ninety-seven.

Betty, of African American heritage, is eighty-eight. Now in a wheelchair following the loss of her leg from complications of illness, she lives with her daughter, who provides her care. Betty was once a dancer at the Apollo Theater in New York City and finds that the memories of earlier days sustain her as she faces a challenging present.

Jane, a European American woman who is ninety-one, recently moved from her home to an assisted living facility at the time of the study. Having survived two husbands, two children, and all her siblings, she wanted to be in a situation where care was available if she needed it. Though well connected to her extended family, Jane still values making her own decisions and maintaining her own life as much as possible.

In addition to these eleven women, you will hear the voices of Dorothy, Carrie, Adel, Bea, and Irene, participants in an earlier study on media images of older women.[34]

We began this chapter with the words of Ann and the experiences of invisibility of Dorothy, Rose, and Jane. Before we can move further toward a model of care to challenge this, we must first understand the social construction of this experience. What are the processes that cause women to fade from our view? To this question we now turn.

CHAPTER 2

The Cultural Construction
of Old Age

Sitting in a blue recliner, Joan appears relaxed and ready to reminisce about her life. With glasses and a stylish short gray hairstyle and pastel striped blouse, Joan seems as if she is in her seventies. When asked, "How do you know when someone is old? What does it mean to be old?" she replies, "I don't think I am." When pressed further to describe someone who is old, she replies:

> Becoming inactive. Getting wrinkles. Oh, I'm getting some of that. An old person…They use a walker or can't walk as they once did and are just not as active. They're inactive. And of course, I am not as active as I used to be, but I don't feel old. And some of these people are old chronologically. Well, that is what I am, but I don't act and feel old.

Joan announces in her gentle Southern manner that she does not feel old because "I think young," and declares that most people are quite surprised that she is eighty-three years old. Staying active by walking regularly and being involved in her assisted living community are ways that Joan strives to keep young and healthy.

As the interviewer continues to ask Joan for clarification, she responds, "You know, that is a hard question." The interviewer continues: "You are not old, and they are not old, but what is the concept of old?"

> I guess just giving up and failing to become a part of other people. You know, that is a hard question. I have said to some people, you will never be old. They continue to think young and remain active and interested. You know, you just

17

have to remain interested in things and people. Well, you know there are younger people who get old.

Joan then describes a fellow resident, an eighty-nine-year-old man who was born blind and was experiencing new limitations due to aging. She says, "He has the most interesting stories to tell abut things that happened in his life. No, he's not really old."

Joan's distinction between chronological age and attitude was common across the interviews. Generally the women tended to identify others, but not themselves, as being old, and associated old age with being infirm or uninterested in life. Some of the definitions of "old" included "being inactive," "getting wrinkles," "losing interest," "being ill." Katherine, a sixty-six-year-old woman, provides a typical answer to the question, "What images do you think most people have of older women?"

> That we are senile—that they are senile, and that a lot of times they are selfish. They want too much attention, too much of their [others'] time, and that they aren't aware of what is going on in the world now, and that they have a sickness. They can't relate to where younger people are. And look at them. They don't know about all these wonderful newfangled things we deal with, the computers and email and things. Surely they are backward.

Many of the women interviewed described aging in negative terms and at the same time distanced themselves from these definitions, as Joan does. How can we understand this phenomenon? Joan's response provides some clues. She complies with the interviewer's persistent attempts to get her to define age and provides an image of age that is consistent with stereotypical images, while simultaneously rejecting these images. She avoids defining age and then resists the assumption that "old" is a neutral descriptive category determined by chronology, an assumption that is implicit in the younger interviewer's questions. She also refuses to be defined by these stereotypical images of aging. She knows that these images are common, but they don't fit her or the people close to her. Her response illumines the power both of the cultural construction of aging and of the resistance to these constructions.

The purpose of this chapter is to provide an analysis of the social construction of aging. Social constructionism holds that what we assume to be real about the world is not a given, nor are facts waiting out there somewhere to be discovered; rather, knowledge, meaning, and our perceptions of the world emerge through social processes and relationships.[1] A social constructionist perspective of aging argues that *old age* is not a neutral term, but reflects cultural assumptions and values. In this perspective the meanings of aging are not simply constructed through interpersonal interaction, but are influenced by larger social structures such as a market economy, public policies enacted by the state, academic disciplines, and various forms of popular culture.[2] Because cultural meanings are constructed, they can be deconstructed and reconstructed. This has particular relevance for our current study, for if the cultural meanings of aging that shape women's experience are primarily negative, these meanings can be changed.

We begin by exploring the concepts central to a social constructionist approach to aging and the process of cultural imperialism that keeps dominant attitudes in place. A historical review of attitudes toward older women and aging provides an understanding of how concepts of aging are constructed. Returning to the contemporary situation, we examine two predominant perspectives on aging, the biomedical model and that of popular culture, through which aging is generally understood in the United States. These two perspectives represent different constructions of age; each emerges from a community of discourse, and each focuses on a particular dimension of aging. The impact of cultural imperialism can be found in the way in which the biomedical model constructs the aging body and popular culture keeps in place stereotypical images of older women.

The Social Construction of Old Women

Older women who both identify negative stereotypes and at the same time distance themselves from them remind us of the mutability of socially constructed concepts. Understanding the social construction of concepts and meanings illumines how these concepts can be changed. Before looking at some manifestations of the social construction of aging, let us first review some basic premises of a social constructivist approach.

A central tenet of the social constructivist position is that facts are not objective realities to be discovered through value-neutral empirical means. Rather, they emerge out of particular language communities and reflect the values of these communities. Concepts such as "old age" are assigned meaning by communities of discourse, such as the medical community; academic disciplines; the state, which designs public policies to serve the elderly; and popular culture. Social constructivists hold that "all forms of naming are socially constructed," including what appear to be such basic biological categories as male/female and young/old.[3]

From a social constructivist perspective, language not only names the world but also creates and shapes the social world in which we live. Our everyday language about the world reflects "taken-for-granted" truths about the world.[4] This commonplace knowledge also functions to maintain cultural boundaries and classifications. Language places order on a chaotic world, but in so doing it also separates and makes distinctions.[5]

For example, one is either old or young, healthy or ill. The term *old* has ambiguous meanings in our culture, and it can be defined in a number of ways. We generally assume an old person is someone who considers herself old. However, research has indicated that older persons resist this definition, as did the women in my study.[6]

What is the process by which certain cultural attitudes become dominant and persist even in the face of individual opposition to them? We saw earlier that when Joan was pressed to define "old" she resorted to culturally accepted images of decline, while distancing herself from these images. How might we understand the processes behind her simultaneous internalization and rejection of these images? The concept of cultural imperialism, as developed by Iris Marion Young, provides a way to understand this phenomenon.

Cultural Imperialism

Cultural imperialism is the process of establishing a dominant group's experience and culture as the norm.[7] This process creates a paradoxical oppression that stereotypes and renders invisible the "deviant" group. Through primary access to "the means of interpretation and communication in a society," the dominant group is able to impose its perspective on society, and thus upon other groups within society.[8] Encounters between the dominant group and other groups can "challenge the dominant group's claims to universality," according to Young.[9] The dominant group responds to these encounters by defining the difference of the other group in terms of "lack and negation" compared with itself and by marking these groups as Other.[10]

Cultural imperialism constructs stereotypical images of older women and renders them simultaneously as Other and invisible.[11] These stereotypes are often attached in some way to the body, making them difficult to deny. Stereotypes become so much a part of the cultural narrative that they often go unnoticed and uncontested or are seen as a reflection of the way things really are. Those experiencing the impact of cultural imperialism find themselves "defined from the outside" by a cluster of meanings that others have assigned to them.[12]

Dorothy, a seventy-two-year-old artist, vividly witnessed to this reality of being rendered both Other and invisible when she reflected on her experience of being ignored by the younger mothers in her grandson's classroom while assisting with a class activity. She did not expect this cool reception and remembered a very different experience when volunteering in her daughter's classroom, when she was younger.

> As you get older you cease to exist in the eyes of some younger people; you become invisible. No one seems interested in who you are or what you do. It is disconcerting. You are still the same vibrant thirty-year-old in your mind. You're still planning your future, working in the present, and being a vital part of the world, but you feel the rest of the world no longer sees you this way. You feel that you are finished, that you don't count—until you get with your peers, then you become a person again.

Undergirding cultural imperialism is binary thinking, which divides the world into either/or, self and Other.[13] Binary thinking divides reality into opposing pairs; something is this and not that. One manifestation of binary thinking is the pattern of dominance and submission, which tends to characterize patriarchal societies. Binary thinking describes members of the nondominant groups as possessing traits opposite to and inferior to those of the dominant group. For example, males historically have been described as possessing the traits of rationality and strength, whereas women are described as emotional and weak. Younger adults are seen as active, vigorous, and flexible, whereas older adults are described as sedentary, decrepit, and rigid. These patterns of thinking are problematic because they do not allow for multiple realities or perspectives. Womanist and feminist scholars argue that this binary, either/or thinking is part of the systemic structure of domination in Western culture that maintains the dominant group's power.[14]

One of the consequences of oppositional thinking is that the dominant group is described as possessing characteristics that are more positively or highly valued in society. The subordinated group possesses traits that are seen as necessary but secondary to or less than those possessed by the dominant group. The consequence of such thinking is the implicit sub-humanity of the subordinate group.

Those who possess the desirable traits—male, young, European American, for example—are seen as the measure and standard of full humanity. This objectification results in the paradoxical situation of the nondominant group being stereotyped and rendered invisible simultaneously.

Because images of aging are constructed, we might expect these to change over time. However, the process of cultural imperialism reinforces certain images. As images persist, we begin to accept these split images of older women as descriptive of reality rather than as the consequence of cultural processes. Through the following historical review of images of older women, we can see how split images of older women are socially constructed and maintained by cultural imperialism.

Historical Images of Older Women and Aging

Contradictory images of older women have been with us for some time. One historical form of binary thinking in Western culture is the split between women as either sexual or spiritual beings.[15] For older women, this split has been manifested in the opposing images of the wise woman and the witch. Current images of older women often reflect these earlier views. For example, the stereotype of the kindly grandmother may echo ancient images of the wise woman, whose wisdom, including healing skills, was used primarily in the care of others, whereas the stereotype of the mean old woman echoes medieval images of the witch.

Wild Women and Witches: Medieval Views of Women

This connection between old women and witches is not accidental. Lois Banner notes that at the height of the witch hunts in the sixteenth and seventeenth centuries, the average age of women accused of witchcraft was between fifty-five and sixty-five.[16] Women were accused of witchcraft because they were seen as violating propriety or challenging social norms. Whereas women who acted in accordance with social expectations might be regarded as spiritual or wise, women who resisted the established order were seen as sinful.

In the early medieval period, the wise woman was often a healer with knowledge of herbal medicine, and her services benefited others.[17] By the fourteenth century, however, any woman who cured illness without studying medicine at a university (which was forbidden to women) was subject to an accusation of witchcraft. Witches were accused of possessing forbidden knowledge and participating in illicit sexual activity.

"Witch" was the designation for women who transgressed acceptable cultural boundaries.[18] These threats to social morality usually had to do with sexuality and power. The major witchcraft manual *Malleus Maleficarum* (1458) stated, "All witchcraft comes from carnal lust, which in women is insatiable."[19] In a religious culture in which sexual activity was legitimate only for the purpose of procreation, the sexuality of older postmenopausal women was seen as deviant and sinful. Menopause was often linked to witchcraft, because menstruation was understood to purge the body of evil humors. Older women who were no longer thus purged were considered easily corrupted by evil. According to Banner, the denigration of women, particularly following menopause, has a long history in Western thought.[20]

Economic factors, as well as sexuality, played a part in accusations of witchcraft. Elizabeth Markson notes that older women were accused of witchcraft because they were either too poor or too rich.[21] In sixteenth- and seventeenth-century Europe, witch hunts "provided a way to eliminate the poor who were too old or too feeble to work."[22] Women of wealth could also be targets, because the property of a wealthy widow was impounded before the trial. As many as two million women, primarily older, widowed, feeble, or poor, were executed in Europe, and in Puritan Massachusetts those accused of witchcraft were most often older single women.[23]

Old Age in Early America

At the same time that older women were accused of witchcraft, those with social standing who embodied spiritual purity sometimes benefited from the belief common in Puritan America that old age and long life were signs of God's favor.[24] Predominant in America in the seventeenth and eighteenth centuries was a religious view of aging as both a time of physical decline and spiritual growth. Thus the reality of loss was linked with the hope of redemption.

A shift from a veneration of older age to a negative bias against elders began about the time of the American Revolution. Older men of status in prerevolutionary America who possessed financial resources were venerated and had considerable social and economic power, though few reached this stage in life.[25] Because power and wealth usually rested in the hands of older men, the young had little choice but to venerate their elders.[26] These positive attitudes toward aging were, however, generally applied only to men of means; the poor, women, and African Americans who reached old age were typically more neglected than venerated.

The status of old women in colonial America was not determined by land ownership or wealth but by her relationships with others. An aging wife maintained her control of the domestic spheres as long as she remained the spouse of the head of the household. Her stature in old age was also increased by possession of the virtues associated with feminine old age, such as "benevolence, dignity, humility, and serenity."[27] Because a woman's status was largely derived from the relationships with her husband, widowhood marked a dramatic change in both financial and social status; the death of her husband usually meant a woman lost her position as head of the household. Her future livelihood was determined by the legal will, which usually allocated a third of the estate, "the dowager's third," to her.[28]

Many widows, however, were not so fortunate and could depend on neither family nor an inheritance. Puritan preacher Cotton Mather encouraged his congregation to see these women as the "needy poor."[29] Older poor women filled the rolls of the church's charities and were the primary recipients of community relief programs.[30] This presents an interesting contemporary parallel to our own situation, in which older women generally outnumber men and are often more dependent on federal assistance programs such as Medicare and Social Security. In both situations, women are seen as needy and dependent.

Nineteenth-Century Views of Aging: Dualism

In the nineteenth century, the aversion to old age grew with the rise of middle-class society.[31] Previously, aging had been understood primarily through religious categories as "an existential problem requiring moral and spiritual commitment."[32] With the development of the scientific management of aging, the existential and spiritual dimensions of aging were lost. Thomas Cole argues that this development was encouraged by "nineteenth century Protestantism's growing commitment to Victorian morality and scientific progress," which undermined the possibility of embracing the paradoxes of later life.[33] In the Victorian mind-set, the possibility of spiritual growth coexisting with loss or physical decline gave way to the opposition between either a "good old age" of productivity or a "bad old age" of indolence and decline. By the late eighteenth and early nineteenth century, a profound shift in Western attitudes toward aging emerged and old age became a scientific problem to be managed through technical means.[34] Victorian moralists split old age into opposing parts: "the 'good old age' of virtue, health, self-reliance, natural death, and salvation; and the 'bad old age' of sin, disease, dependency, premature death, and damnation."[35] This Victorian morality promised the preservation of health and independence and a good old age to those who worked hard and were faithful and self-disciplined. Premature death or "miserable old age" was the fate of those who were "faithless, shiftless, and promiscuous."[36] Cole suggests that both health reformers and romantic evangelicals contributed to the development and promotion of these ideas.[37]

The emerging technical rationality of the nineteenth century led to the scientific management of aging, as physicians became increasingly interested in old age. An unfortunate consequence of this development for women was the definition of female reproduction as a pathological process. The concept of "climacteric illness," which associated menopause with a decline in mental and physical health, came into being at this time.[38] The diagnosis of hysteria, which also linked mental instability to menopause, also emerged during this period. This medicalization of menopause continues to be reflected in contemporary medicine. The widespread use of hormone therapy to treat menopause (increasingly discredited by new research findings) echoes this pathological approach.

Resistance to this pathological view of women and women's bodies arose with the first wave of the women's movement in the late nineteenth and early twentieth centuries. Many leaders of the women's movement, including Susan B. Anthony, Elizabeth Cady Stanton, and Frances Willard, continued in their roles well into their sixties.[39] Their vital leadership and presence provided alternative images of older women.

At the turn of the twentieth century, aging began to be seen as a problem that required social intervention, although changes appeared as early as the eighteenth century, such as the first mandatory retirements for public officials at a predetermined age, usually sixty or seventy.[40] In 1909 the first public commission on aging was appointed and the first federal pension bill was approved. In the early part of the century, a significant number of the elderly faced severe poverty and ill health. The economic situation improved tremendously for many older Americans after the passage of the Social Security Act in 1935. However, not all older adults have benefited equally from these changes. Older women, African Americans, Hispanics, and members of other immigrant groups who have been outside of regular employment structures still face significant poverty in old age. The Older Americans Act of 1965 established the Administration on Aging within the Department of Health, Education, and Welfare and called for the creation of state units on aging. The

Administration on Aging has enabled the development of many services, including low-income housing, meal programs, and transportation services that have significantly improved the material conditions of many older adults. Images and attitudes, however, change more slowly.

The process of cultural imperialism, with its underlying structure of binary thinking, can be seen in both historical and contemporary perspectives on aging. Although the current dominant perspectives on aging are rooted in earlier historical images, they also reflect contemporary developments, such as technological advances in medicine and the influence of mass media.

Contemporary Models of Aging

Although we could identify many perspectives on aging, two—the biomedical and popular cultural notions—function as the dominant perspectives in the contemporary United States. Each of these approaches is constructed, arising out of a particular community of discourse and reflecting its values, and each focuses on certain dimensions of aging. The biomedical model of aging focuses on the physical, bodily experience of aging. A secondary consequence of the biomedical model is the way in which it shapes aging policy, particularly benefit programs such as Medicare. Popular cultural definitions of aging, which see aging as a period of decline, are maintained through images, stereotypes, stories, myths, and media. For example, it is common to find birthday cards making fun of old age, adorned with the image of a grumpy old woman. A shared element among these perspectives is a tendency toward binary thinking that defines the world in terms of opposites such as old/young, male/female, healthy/ill, and dependent/independent. This binary thinking leads to opposite images of good and bad old age, thus obscuring the ambiguities of aging and the varieties of experience.

If we perceive aging primarily in biological terms, we are quite likely to see aging in terms of its physical manifestations. Elizabeth Binney and Carroll Estes posit that the medical model views aging as a period of physical decline or an illness state that requires treatment.[41] They argue that this biomedical model has led to social images of aging as a pathological process. Although much good has come out of biomedical research on aging and the diseases that often occur in late life, an unintended consequence is that old age becomes an undesirable condition associated with infirmity: a condition to be cured, not embraced. These attitudes are reflected in Joan's comments about what it means to be old.

A secondary consequence of the biomedical model is its influence in shaping social programs such as Medicare. Although these programs have improved the quality of life for many persons, Haim Hazan points out that the biomedical perspective tends to define older adults in terms of needs.[42] He claims, "There is a tendency, especially among those engaged in the provision of welfare services for the aged, to see them as a mass of material exigencies."[43] Unfortunately, the unintended consequence is a tendency to patronize older adults or to see them as "greedy geezers," consuming all the public resources.[44]

Popular culture constructs and maintains a second perspective of aging as a period of unremitting decline. Influences of the biomedical model are present in the popular definitions of aging. In addition, this definition is shaped by media images of older women (or the lack of them) and is communicated in social stereotypes, some of which are deeply rooted.[45] Hazan argues that one of the most common stereotypes of the elderly is that "they are conservative, inflexible and resistant to change."[46] Older adults are not expected to grow and change, much less learn. Thus when older adults take on a new challenge such as learning computer skills or getting an advanced degree at the age of seventy or above, it is a newsworthy story because this must be the exception.[47]

The Biomedical Model of Aging

The ideal of the healthy, strong young body emerged in the United States and Europe in the nineteenth century. The image of a good old age was associated with the continuity of strength and vitality, whereas "bad" old age was associated with disease and physical frailties, which were also seen as manifestations of moral weakness. In the framework of this binary approach to age, women were "considered delicate and weak due to the specific constitution of their bodies" and their reproductive systems.[48]

At this point, "a general medical and cultural association between old age and disease, degeneracy, and death" begins to appear.[49] The degeneracy of age is evident in the "ugliness of old people, especially old women."[50] Such attitudes toward aging bodies generally operate at an unconscious level but are often perpetuated through stereotypes or media images. This association of old age with physical decline was also evident in the interviews, as exemplified by Joan's comments reported earlier.

The biomedical model "emphasizes the etiology, clinical treatment, and management of diseases of the elderly as defined and treated by medical practitioners, while giving marginal attention to the social and behavioral process and problems of aging."[51] The consequence of linking old age and illness are social attitudes toward aging as "pathological, abnormal, and an undesirable state."[52] Aging, then, becomes a curable condition. Such a perspective shapes not only academic thinking and research but also popular culture. For example, on the cover of the October 2002 *Reader's Digest* magazine appears the headline "The New Cure for Aging." In the opening paragraph of the article, reporting on recent medical advances, are these words: "Astounding breakthroughs offer a cure for aging...Biomedicine promises to defeat disease of all sorts, if not death itself."[53]

If age is defined as a medical condition, older persons become "patients." The biomedical model reinforces images of the elderly as dependent and sick. Such perceptions may influence the behavior of older persons, encouraging them to act sick and dependent. The solution then is to become a consumer of high-cost medical services and technology.[54] The elderly and the larger public accept the definition of aging as largely a biological condition and thus overlook the socially constructed images and problems of aging. These perceptions lead to social policies in which dependent elderly are to be managed by professionals who understand these medical processes.

The medical model of aging has political consequences, because the medical profession has a monopoly on any condition that requires medical treatment.[55] Estes and her colleagues have identified two key elements in the biomedicalization of aging: (1) thinking of aging in terms of a condition to be treated and (2) aging as a medical problem that gives rise to certain procedures and policies.[56] The medical model is so influential that it obscures the influence of other social factors, such as income and education, that also contribute to issues faced by the elderly.[57]

One of the unintended consequences of the biomedicalization of aging is its contribution to the social construction of dependency in the elderly. Critical gerontologists argue that dependency in the elderly is a "social product."[58] A multitude of forces contribute to the social construction of dependency. The power differentials and social relations between older persons and the professional caregivers who provide services may produce dependency. These power inequities can be seen in nursing homes and other settings where residents have to accommodate to the needs and schedules of the care providers. Such created dependency may result in a distortion of care in which the one cared for becomes an object to be managed rather than a subject.

When another person is seen as an object of care, the care given is often designed to fit the needs of the caregiver, such as convenience of schedule. While doing research in nursing homes in the summer of 1997, I was impressed with the quality of care in many of the institutions I visited. At the same time I also observed that even in the best institutions the approach to residents was that of management. Problem residents needed to be "managed," and schedules and needs of the institution often took precedence over the individual needs and subjective experiences of the residents. For example, Ida, a ninety-two-year-old woman who was relatively new to the facility and restricted in her mobility, was described to me as a "problem," because she often complained about the food. Ida did complain about the food in her conversations with me, but her complaints seemed to be the result of giving up control in the one area in her life in which she could still exercise some agency: choosing what to eat. Prior to coming to the nursing home, Ida had been relatively independent. Because the category of interdependency was not available to her, the only other choice was to be defined as completely dependent on the care providers, a definition she resisted. I wondered if the situation could be resolved by involving her in meal planning, at least giving her some choices, even if from a relatively fixed menu, and thus returning some sense of agency to her.

Aging and Death

The biomedicalization of aging has also led to the association of aging with death. In earlier historical periods, death could be expected at any point in life, and because the young were as likely to die as the old, survival to old age was seen as a sign of divine favor. With advances in medicine, infant mortality rates have dropped and we expect death to come at the end of life. When it does not, we consider the death untimely. Older adults are thus seen to be on the boundary between life and death.[59] By distancing ourselves from the elderly, by seeing them as fundamentally different from ourselves, we can distance ourselves from death.[60] For many, old age and its presumed fragility and senility are a cruel joke. A cartoon in a recent *New Yorker* magazine depicted a middle-aged man clinging to a parking meter with a desperate look on his face, shouting, "More quarters! For God's sake more quarters!" The parking meter was marked "youth" on one end and "senility" on the other, and time was quickly running out.[61]

This association of age with senility and death is reflected in our deep cultural ambivalence toward aging and toward aged persons. The elderly elicit our deepest fears—that we are indeed vulnerable and that we will die. Although it may be images of the frail elderly that trigger these fears, even the well elderly remind us that we will not be always be in the favored position of the young. The very existence of older adults reminds us that our lives too will end. We do not want to admit that "work ends, health fails, and sooner or later, even love dies."[62] Because we are a culture focused on the future, we "fear those whose lives speak too forcefully of what has been."[63]

In an effort to deny our own aging, we simply do not see the seniors around us. They become invisible. Tom Koch powerfully captures this aversion to aging and to the older adults who remind us of its inevitability:

> We do not like our seniors, nor do we understand them. They are wrinkled, shrunken in stature, and too often speak in dry and querulous voices. Our assumptions of physical beauty and social responsibility are violated by the elderly, who rarely work and are free of the obligations that plague us younger adults. Like ungainly, assertive adolescents, retirees are frustrating and vexing challenges to the model of adulthood that society holds dear.[64]

If old age becomes the repository for our fear of death and the rejection of our mortality, then we can begin to understand Joan's impulse and our own to distance ourselves from aging and aged persons.

Popular Culture

Images of the body also play a central role in popular culture. When making judgments about whether someone is old or young, we usually do so by looking at the body. We notice the texture of the skin, the color of the hair, gait, and posture. It is from the body, and particularly the face, that we "draw conclusions about a person's age, sex, race, ability, and health."[65] If we know someone is "old" according to the social definition of old, but the person's appearance does not match our expectation, we rarely challenge our assumptions of age, but declare that this particular individual appears young for her age. These visual cues are not neutral "facts" that we gather about someone's age, but are interpreted through our culturally shaped assumptions.

Studies examining the link between social perceptions and facial appearance have demonstrated that different characteristics or stereotypes are assigned to faces based on apparent age.[66] In one study, young adults were asked to pair twenty-four photographs selected earlier by participants as representing older persons with a set of traits describing ten stereotypes of elderly adults. These stereotypes had arisen from an earlier study by the same researcher. Persons identified as the young-old (fifty-five to sixty-five in this research) were more likely paired with positive stereotypes, and the old-old (seventy-five and older) were more often paired with negative stereotypes. These findings were generally true for women and men, though older women in all categories were more often associated with negative stereotypes than men, suggesting that physical cues of advanced old age lead to more negative perception of women than men.[67]

This practice of distinguishing ourselves from others through bodily appearance is a manifestation of cultural imperialism. The nondominant group is distanced, in part through aversion, which is based on a construction of the oppressed group's body as ugly. Those defined as different are imprisoned in bodies judged to be "dirty, defiled, impure, contaminated, or sick."[68] Young argues that both old and disabled people, as well as people of color, "also occupy as groups the position of ugly, fearful, or loathsome bodies."[69]

Various forms of media serve as primary mechanisms of popular culture that communicate images of older women—or the lack of them. One indication of the invisibility of older women is the paucity of images of older women in the media. Few older women appear in major motion pictures or prime-time television shows. Images of older women are likewise scarce in fashion magazines, advertisements, and most print media. Given the size of the population of older women and the breadth of ages represented, we should expect a complex depiction of older women that would allow for the heterogeneity and diversity of the population.

A review of prime-time network programming in the 1990s indicated that only 3 percent of characters, both male and female, in major and supporting roles, could be categorized as elderly. In contrast, 7 percent of the characters are children, 36 percent are young adults, and 53 percent are middle-aged. In addition, when women were present, they were portrayed as five years younger than their male counterparts, except in the case of elderly women, who were portrayed as a year older than the men. A gender difference also appears in characters categorized as elderly. Only one in ten men between fifty and sixty-four were categorized as elderly, whereas 22 percent of women in the same age range were presented as elderly. This discrepancy was also evident for those judged to be sixty-five or older; 75 percent of the men and 83 percent of the women were categorized as elderly. Overall, the findings of this study indicate that the primary message on television is one that celebrates youth and marginalizes the elderly.[70]

Women in films do not fare much better. In 1999 the Screen Actors' Guild reported that only one in three roles went to performers over forty, with women being less likely to be cast than men (24 percent for women compared with 37 percent for men). In an analysis of the Academy Awards over sixty-three years (1927 to 1990), only one in five of all female nominees for Best Actress was over the age of thirty-nine, compared with more than 50 percent for the men.[71] In films, women are more often portrayed in stereotypically feminine roles, such as housewives, nannies, or shopkeepers, than in professional roles.[72] Women are also more likely to be portrayed in relationship to men than to each other in popular films.[73]

We noted in our earlier discussion of women accused of witchcraft that women's sexuality has often been seen as problematic or dangerous, and this is true of media representations of women as well. Marilyn Maxwell's analysis of fictional characters in literature demonstrated that postmenopausal women were described as sexually voracious.[74] The implicit message of the 1950s film *Sunset Boulevard* is that Norma Desmond's needs and sexual desire are fatal to the young man who falls into her clutches. It is interesting to note that although Norma is portrayed as aging, and living in a world out of time, the film reveals her as being fifty years old. Clearly old age comes early for women in film.

Given the increase in the older population and the potential market it represents, we might expect to see an increasing number of print advertisements directed to and depicting older adults. However, Judith de Luce found in her review of magazines generally available at newsstands that so little attention was paid to fifty-plus consumers that they were virtually invisible.[75] Of the thirty-one magazines reviewed, three contained eleven to fifteen ads that either appealed to or represented readers over the age of fifty. Four included six to ten ads, nineteen offered one to five ads, and four offered no such ads. De Luce's findings echo the voices of women I interviewed who generally do not see themselves in the pages of the magazines they often read, with the exception of those directed toward an older population, such as publications of the American Association of Retired Persons.

What images of older women do older women themselves notice in the media? I asked this question in an earlier interview study (1997) of older widows.[76] Many of the respondents noted that they did not see many images of older women, and those images that were present portrayed stereotypical images that did not reflect the women's lives.

Adel, age sixty-six, noted that clothing ads rarely depict older women. She thought it was condescending for department stores to assume that only young women need to dress up. She comments, "Women my age dress up a lot more than twenty-somethings. They'd probably sell more dresses if they showed women my age. But you won't catch an advertisement with real women in it; they're afraid to show us." Adel also found advertisements for liquid nutritional supplements demeaning to older women:

> They imply that older people are too ignorant to eat nutritious foods. I don't know anyone who drinks that stuff. We don't need food supplements, just a good balanced diet. People my age have good appetites. Just look in the restaurants. Everywhere you look you see senior citizens. We're the ones with the money; they should be courting us!

These responses confirm the findings of Patricia Miller, who conducted a review of stereotypes of the elderly in magazine advertisements from 1956 to 1996. Miller and her associates showed that the portrayal of elderly persons in print ads had decreased, while the elderly population had increased. Although only 4 percent of the ads used negative stereotypes, this still represented an increase in negative stereotypes and a decrease in positive images.[77]

Of the ten respondents who answered the questions about media, television was the medium most often mentioned, over films and magazines. The majority of women found that their own experience was not reflected back to them through the television, and about one-third of the women did not watch much television, in part because the shows seemed irrelevant to their lives. Bea, seventy-nine, said that TV commentators "put older people down" and portrayed them as weak or frail. Although this was not entirely clear from the interviews, the absence of older women on television may have contributed to this sense of irrelevancy.

Several of the respondents specifically mentioned the television show *The Golden Girls,* which aired from 1985 to 1992 and continues in reruns, although reactions to the show varied. Irene, a sixty-six-year-old married woman shared one typical response. "Those women weren't like the women I know. They have a lot of boyfriends and go out; I do most of my 'stuff' through the church. *Golden Girls* never showed women going to church." A negative response also is present in the comments of Carrie, a ninety-one-year-old working-class woman who also describes herself as "French American Indian," is widowed, and lives alone in the rural Midwest.

> At first I really liked that show. But after a while I started not liking the way the mother acted–she was just plain mean sometimes. She acted all smart-alecky and nasty and forgetful. And at first it was kind of funny because she wasn't saying those things on purpose. You see, she'd had a stroke and couldn't always know what she said. And I enjoyed the parts where she came up with ways to keep her independence, like sitting on two or three phone books to drive! But later on, she just got so mean, and her daughter treated her like a little child so often that I just had to stop watching.

Carrie also found that television generally portrayed widowed women, such as herself, in a negative light:

> I think that T.V. shows widows pretty much like they do old women…being forgetful and impatient. But they also show them needing help all the time. Like if there is no man in the house, the woman can't do anything by herself. The other thing I think of is that they show widows as bitter or angry. Like if there is a Halloween show, some old woman is in a spooky house, and all the kids are scared of her–it is always a mean, angry, very strange widow woman. There is never a husband in those houses, only an alone woman.

Carrie's comments reflect the view we observed earlier, of the persistence of opposing images of older women as either helpless or dangerous and mean and witchlike.

In our earlier historical survey we noted the presence of the opposing images of the wise woman or witch in medieval culture, although antecedents of these images appear earlier.[78] I believe that the wise old woman has been transformed into the "little old lady." Rose, whom we met in chapter 1, cites the "little old lady syndrome" when explaining her experience of being ignored by the younger women working next to her at a church event. Rose comments that the two women who ignored her "did have a stereotypical image." In this encounter we can see how stereotypes render older women both as Other and as invisible. The young women were sharing with each other their surprisingly enjoyable encounters with older women, while Rose was invisible to them. Rose judges their surprise as manifestations of their stereotypical assumptions about these women. Rose notes, "Little old ladies just don't really seem to count for much to a lot of people." Little old ladies are sweet, nonconfrontational, proper, polite, and asexual.

A variation of the little old lady image is the grandmother. These images reduce the agency of older women and render them powerless and harmless. The stereotypical grandmother is in the kitchen baking cookies for her grandchildren. Implicit in this image is the assumption that she exists solely for the nurture of others and has no needs of her own. At this point we can see a faint shadow of the wise woman, whose wisdom was harmless as long as it was in the service of others.

Gerontologists have tried to identify stereotypes of the elderly through structured research. In a 1990 study of young adults, Mary Lee Hummert identified three positive stereotypes: the perfect grandparent, the liberal matriarch/patriarch, and the John Wayne conservative.[79] Some stereotypes were more likely to be assigned to one gender over the other; for example, the perfect grandmother occurred more often than the perfect grandfather, and the John Wayne type was more associated with men. The negative stereotypes included the severely impaired; the inflexible senior citizen; self-centered, recluse, despondent, shrew/curmudgeon, and vulnerable senior citizens. Studies by Smith and Boland (1986) resulted in a similar grouping of stereotypes.[80] These studies confirm the presence of the opposing images of the sweet grandmother, perceived as kind, trustworthy, loving, family oriented, and generous, and the old woman as shrew, who is complaining, bitter, ill-tempered, selfish, and stubborn.[81]

Although African American women are also sometimes stereotyped as sweet little old ladies or as mean old women, Patricia Hill Collins argues that black women face unique stereotypes, such as mammy and Jezebel, that represent the "intersecting oppressions of race, gender, sexuality, and class."[82] The stereotypical mammy is asexual and exists for the nurture of others, but these others are white children, not her own. Unlike the little old lady image, embedded in the image of the mammy are both racial oppression and economic exploitation. Hill Collins argues that the Jezebel is the sexualized image of black women that functions to control black women's sexuality.[83] The image of Jezebel constructs black women as hypersexual. This sexuality, which is seen by the white culture as dangerous, is thus controlled and marginalized through this image.[84] Similar to the witch image, the Jezebel image represented sexually aggressive women. Just as the accusation of witch condoned violence to women seen as sexually deviant, the image of Jezebel "provided a rationale for the widespread assaults by White men typically reported by black slave women."[85]

Such stereotypes, as Young notes, are a manifestation of cultural imperialism that renders women as both invisible and Other. Stereotypes are not intended to be an objective representation of reality, but rather to obscure social relations and serve as a means of social control.[86] Stereotypes normalize oppression, making it appear natural, and they reduce the complexity of real persons to caricatures. Thus stereotypes point to the "Otherness" of older women.

Through our review of historical and contemporary perspectives on aging we can see how images of older women are constructed, arising out of particular communities of discourse such as medicine or popular culture. We have also seen how cultural imperialism and binary thinking maintain stereotypical images of older women. Although the content of the images may change somewhat, the processes that simultaneously support these cultural stereotypes and render women Other persist.

An Alternative Perspective

Is it possible to conceive of other models of aging available to us beside the images present in popular culture or the biomedical model? Two key developments are necessary to the articulation of an alternative model. First we must move beyond the dualism implicit in the predominant models of aging, and second, we must move beyond the individualistic approach to aging underlying these models.

Another model of aging has existed alongside of, but often in the shadow of, these two other images. It is the model of aging as a time of spiritual growth or journey. In this model, old age still presents opportunities for spiritual and emotional growth, even in the midst of losses or health challenges. The image of age as a time of spiritual growth is evident in the Christian tradition, particularly in earlier historical periods. In Puritan theology of the seventeenth century, life was seen as an ongoing journey toward salvation. Behind this perspective was a biblically inspired assumption that, regardless of age, no one is a fully completed person, because no one, regardless of age, can reach full maturity in Christ through human effort alone. As a result, all ages are equal in God's eyes, and human beings are capable of spiritual growth irrespective of age.[87] This vision of aging reflected Augustine's understanding of Christian life as journey or voyage home.[88]

Thomas Cole notes that the cultural dominance of the scientific and medical models of aging that emerged in the nineteenth century is beginning to wane. Perhaps the time is ripe, then, to reclaim some of the wisdom of earlier religious visions of aging that saw it as part of a life journey and that embraced the ambiguities of aging.[89] Indeed, some contemporary authors have reclaimed this vision of aging and have begun paying more attention to the spiritual dimensions of aging.[90] Rather than splitting old age into opposing images of good, healthy old age and bad, diseased old age, or older women into categories of good sweet grandmothers or mean old shrews, perhaps we can find a way of embracing the ambiguity of our embodied, finite, human existence. This task, however, requires more than new personal interpretations of aging. It calls for communities and communal practices that can sustain an alternative theological approach. In the next chapter we will turn our attention to these communities and the practices of care that might arise from them.

CHAPTER 3

Challenging Invisibility
An Ecclesial Vision and Practices of Care

It's Sunday morning and worship services are beginning in various churches across town. Let's slip into the pews of a few of these congregations.[1]

Sarah opens her worship bulletin and finds an invitation to list her gifts and talents and how she might use these in her church's ministry. As she reflects on her recent experience, she wonders if what she says on her list will make much difference to anybody. For many years she had been an active leader in her church and was often asked to chair committees or serve in other positions of leadership. She found these opportunities a meaningful way to serve her church and live out her faith, as well as an affirmation of her gifts of leadership, something she did not experience as much in her professional life. But since her retirement she has been asked less often by the church to serve in positions of leadership. Somehow, it seems that others see her as less competent now that she has retired, although she herself feels no different.

Katherine enjoys her new church home, which she found after a careful search following her move upon retirement to be closer to her children and grandchildren. She has found a community of like-minded folks of various races and cultures who share her conviction regarding the importance of recognizing and bridging difference. She feels particularly at home in the Sunday school class composed mostly of people in her own age group who seem to understand the complexity of her identity and her life. She enjoys her work with the refugee family her Sunday school class has "adopted" to ease its transition into an unfamiliar society. This experience provides her with many opportunities for learning and growth. Yet despite all these positive experiences, she feels the divide of generational differences, particularly with the younger women in her church. The young associate pastor seems much like her daughter: kind and respectful but not convinced that Katherine has much to say to her that is relevant. Katherine knows she is much more than a cookie-baking grandma, which is how she feels younger women in the church, including the associate pastor, see her.

Julie opens the hymnal to a favorite tune as she waits for the service to begin in the retirement home where she now lives. She thinks about her home church, which she can no longer attend, and wonders what she would have done without the help of that community in the past few years. She did not feel old until she had to cope with so many changes after the death of her second husband. Chief among those changes was being forced to leave the home in which she and her husband had been living, because it belonged to her stepson. With few options and few financial resources after the loss of her husband's pension income, she did not know what to do. Although her husband had planned for her to go to a retirement home affiliated with a service organization of which he had been a part, it was far away from her home, her friends, and her church. Proud of her independence, and reluctant to confide in her friends, she finally turned to her pastor, who helped her find a placement in a church-related retirement home in the area. Although she can no longer attend, her church still helps her a bit financially when she is in need, and members who have been long-time friends still stay in touch. She does not know what she would have done without the help of the church. Deeply appreciative of that help but ashamed of her dependence, she has kept her financial problems a secret from the other residents in her building. As she looks around at the other worshipers beside her, she is glad that few of them know her story.

Assessing the Issues, Broadening Our Perspective

Sarah, Katherine, and Julie are like many older women in our congregations, each uniquely facing the opportunities and challenges of life. To some extent each of them has found the congregation a meaningful community in which to live out their Christian faith, and these congregations have provided support for this vocation. At the same time, as we can see in these stories, many congregations are influenced by a cultural context that does not value aging or older women, and unfortunately such attitudes often influence the church's ministry with these women. How might we discern the ways in which the cultural construction of age and "older woman" unintentionally shapes the practices of ministry in various churches? Let's revisit each of these stories.

Sarah is coming to terms with retirement and exploring vocation in new ways. Yet cultural ambivalence toward and marginalization of retirees who are no longer productive seems to be operative in her local church. Sarah faced a mandatory retirement age based not on her ability to contribute to society but on her age. Unfortunately, it appears that stereotypical views of retirees influenced her church's practice of leadership selection, and consequently Sarah now feels marginalized in her congregation.

Katherine is adjusting well to a move to a new community in order to be closer to her children and grandchildren and has found a church in which she can be involved. Yet she feels she does not fit the stereotypical images of older women assigned to her. She feels constricted by images of what a grandmother should do or be, but tends to see this as a personal issue that she must work out in her relationships. It is not clear that Katherine's pastor or congregation are aware of the way in which these images shape their perceptions of Katherine and impose unwanted limits on her.

Julie is dealing with the loss of her husband and her home, as well as significant economic challenges. She is fortunate in belonging to a church that has taken some responsibility for her care, even though she can no longer attend because of her move. Yet as Julie tells her story, it is clear that she feels that her situation is a consequence of poor choices she and her husband made and her inability to provide for herself. Although there may be some truth in this assessment, larger systemic forces have contributed to Julie's situation. Having fulfilled the expected role of wife rather than income-earning professional, Julie has few economic resources of her own. Julie is ashamed of the economic dependence in which she finds herself, because her self-image is of a responsible, hard-working person. Neither Julie nor the church seems fully aware of the way in which her dependence has been constructed by larger social forces.

The stories of Sarah, Katherine, and Julie illustrate the ways in which the cultural construction of aging affects our practices of care in congregations. Recognition of these influences can help reframe the approach to ministry with older women so that care of older women becomes less concerned with solving the "problem" of aging than with understanding and valuing the complexity and uniqueness of each woman's life.

As we saw in the previous chapter, cultural imperialism tends to construct old age as a problem to be solved. This can result in older women being viewed as a problem. The dominant models of aging, the biomedical and popular cultural images, maintain this perspective on aging. Often these images unconsciously influence older women's self-perceptions, and congregational practices that also reflect the dominant view can reinforce these self-perceptions.

How can we help congregations recognize the impact of the cultural construction of aging, offer an alternative view of older women, and become good places to grow old? What models and practices of care can facilitate this process? The first step toward our goal is conducting a critical social analysis, as we did in the previous chapter. This analysis helps identify the models and images of aging that shape practice. The process of cultural imperialism often makes the influences of these models hard to identify. Because they are so pervasive, we assume that that is just the way it is and we are unaware of the construction of these images. The second step is returning to the Christian tradition to see how a theology of aging might challenge the biomedical model and the stereotypical images of popular culture. The third step is to reflect on congregational life and to articulate an ecclesiology that supports this theological model of aging and fosters interdependence, mutuality, and care. This leads to the fourth step: the development of both our theory and practices of care through which congregations can be communities in which we journey together through life, in all its ages and stages. Such communities can then affirm the gifts of older women and challenge their invisibility.

A Theological Model of Aging

The dominant models of aging assume that human beings are autonomous individuals and that the goal of healthy development is independence. From this framework, aging is seen primarily as an individual experience. This assumption is evident in the biomedical model's conception of human beings as individual biological organisms and is reflected in images of older adults as dependent and in need of care by the state or by younger independent adults. Undergirding this stereotype is the binary opposition of dependence, defined as a failure of autonomy, and independence, the desired state in which one is self-sufficient.

A Relational Anthropology

An alternative view of aging must begin with a different anthropology or set of assumptions about the nature of human beings. Beginning with a theological anthropology that sees human beings as relational rather than autonomous can lead to a new understanding of aging.[2] A relational theological anthropology begins with the affirmation that human beings are created in the image of the Triune God. Informing this anthropology is a doctrine of the Trinity in which the three Persons are seen primarily in terms of their relationships with one another rather than in terms of their substance or absolute, individual characteristics.[3] Human beings are created in the image of this relational God and are thus also understood as persons-in-relation. We are created in and for relationship with the Divine, other human beings, and the whole of creation, rather than as autonomous or independent creatures.

A relational Trinitarian anthropology affirms that human beings are both unique individuals and social beings. Our uniqueness is rooted in God's relationship to each one of us, and at the same time we are embedded in a relational and social web through which our personhood is realized.[4] Although God constitutes our personhood as human beings, we come to know our individual sense of self through our relationships with other persons.[5] Miroslav Volf proclaims this reality in bold words.

> Hence, even though every human being is constituted in his or her personhood by God, that person's inner "makeup" is still that of a social and natural being. Without other human beings, even God cannot create a human being! Even if God were to create an isolated being, that being would not be a human being.[6]

To be human, then, is to be constituted by relationships with God and other persons.

The binary opposition of dependence and independence is challenged by a relational anthropology. The reality of human existence is interdependence; we cannot exist apart from each other. From the perspective of autonomy, we define dependence as weakness or incompleteness. For example, we tend to see infants, who are by nature dependent, in need of care and not yet autonomous, as not yet a self, and thus not fully human. Similarly, older adults, who through frailty or illness might be dependent, are also defined as not fully human, because one's humanity has been diminished by a return to dependence. In the case of dependent older adults, however, it is assumed that there is no potential for future development of autonomy and full selfhood, as is the case with infants. These assumptions are challenged by a relational anthropology that claims that by our very nature we are interdependent. At various times we may need more or less care from others, but the truth is that we are never truly independent.

Beginning with a relational anthropology allows us to recognize that aging is not just an individual process; it is also an interpersonal and social process. How we age affects others around us as well. K. Brynolf Lyon refers to this social dimension of aging as the "relational ground of the moral praxis of aging."[7] This relational moral praxis of aging, Lyon argues, is a central dimension of the Christian tradition's perspective on aging. Lyon reconstructs this perspective through a historical review of theological teaching on aging, attending to figures such as Chrysostom, Augustine, Ambrose, Jerome, John Calvin, and Richard Baxter. Lyon asserts that this historical Christian perspective understands old age as a blessing from God. As such, this time in one's life is to be a time of spiritual growth in which one continues to move toward a right relationship with God.[8] Such right relationship, however, is not simply a private matter but presumed right relationship with one's neighbor.

Older adults are thus called to a particular "religioethical witness that is expressed through a moral praxis of aging."[9] This moral praxis includes care for subsequent generations, as well as care for oneself. Within this Christian tradition, aging is understood to have a relational and communal dimension, as opposed to being simply an individual phenomenon. One's spiritual growth and self-fulfillment are inextricably linked to the care of others.[10] Older adults cannot accomplish this on their own; rather, "the community itself must encourage and sustain the care and contribution of older adults."[11] Christian communal life is enriched or diminished by the way in which it cares for and receives the care of older adults.

The Christian theological tradition provides an alternative model of aging that views late life not as a period of decline but as a time of continued spiritual growth, even in the midst of losses that might accompany aging. Thus we are invited to claim the ambiguity of our creaturely existence, which embraces both growth and loss, and to affirm God's presence with us in the midst of this embodied life. Elders are also called to claim a particular vocation of caring for self and others.

This theological vision sees aging as more than an individual endeavor and requires the community of faith to bear a countercultural witness about aging as a part of human life in the face of cultural notions that would oppose such a view. In order for older women to live out such a vocation of aging, however, the Christian community also must value the contributions of older women and become communities that sustain the moral praxis of aging.

Challenging Individualism in the Church

Moving toward a theological model of aging also requires that we think about our understanding of the church. Our anthropology and models of aging have been individualistic, as we saw in the case of Julie, who largely blames herself for the situation in which she finds herself. Our ecclesiology also reflects this cultural value. The charge of individualism has been leveled against the church, as well as the larger American culture.[12] The old-line Protestant churches not only have faced continued membership and financial decline but also have had to contend with accusations of spiritual decline, "internal critiques of its theological and practical individualism, and challenges to its missions of charity rather than justice."[13] Peter Hodgson speaks of individualism and privatism as contemporary perversion of the church.[14] He is critical of both liberal and conservative Protestants, arguing that both have tended to see religion as a matter of private piety or humanistic ideals.[15]

When religion becomes privatized, the communal dimensions of the church are minimized and we lose sight of what the church is and can be.[16] As a consequence, we expect the church to be primarily "a means of satisfying private, therapeutic needs."[17] According to Hodgson, this results in "questions of truth and redemptive community" being replaced by a concern for the successful adjustment of individuals to the challenges of life.[18] Such privatization of religious life leads us to question the necessity of the church, as other institutions could satisfy these needs.

Thus it is clear to me that we need a vision of the church that challenges individualism and values community while maintaining a dynamic interplay between individuality and connection. This vision of the church connects a relational anthropology with a relational ecclesiology. Such an ecclesiology is needed in order to sustain a theological model of aging, which affirms the communal dimensions of aging, promotes an understanding of aging as "moral praxis," and challenges older women's invisibility.

Why does our vision of the church matter to our ministry with older women? Why not just get down to the strategies of what we are to do with older women? For one thing, when we frame the question this way, we once again see older women as a problem to be solved. Second, all practices are theory-laden.[19] This means that whatever practices we employ in our ministry with older women will imply some model of care and some vision of the church. Will these implicit models of care and church fit our understanding of aging, and will these models serve the flourishing of older women?

Third, who we are, or understand ourselves to be, shapes what we do. Our identity as a community of faith shapes our practices. For example, if we understand ourselves primarily as a community of autonomous individuals, our worship practices will support the development of individual piety and a sense of independence from other worshipers. In this situation, private prayer and devotion become the norm. If, however, we understand ourselves to be a community of persons who are essentially relational beings, we are called to practices that celebrate our interdependence. This might mean that we take praying for one another and communal prayer as central to our prayer life.

A Vision of the Church: A Widening Circle of Gracious Inclusion

I propose a vision of the church as an ever-widening circle of gracious inclusion that assumes a relational anthropology and is built upon an ecclesiology of koinonia (communion). A vision of the church as an ever-widening circle of inclusion can foster the flourishing of older women and challenge the invisibility of older women in church and society. An ecclesiology of koinonia defines the church as a "web of interwoven relationships" and understands the nature and purpose of the Christian community as sharing in the life and love of the triune God.[20] The inner life of the Trinity, which includes both individuality and relationship, provides the analogy for relationships within the church.

The vision of church as a widening circle has two dimensions. Although the circle contains, supports, and upholds its members, it also opens its arms to include and embrace those who are excluded, marginalized, or invisible. These two dimensions of holding and inclusion are simultaneous and extend both to those who have been a part of the church for some time and to those who are new to it.[21] Envisioning the church in this way highlights our relationship to each other and our interdependence as members of one community of faith. It is through God's inclusive embrace of us that we are enabled to embrace others. We are held in the ever-widening circle of God's grace and called to embody this grace in our communities of faith and congregational life.

Widening the circle means challenging the marginalization and invisibility of older women in order to value their presence and contributions to church life more consciously. Their contributions and life stories are an important part of who we are as a community of faith. This means more than just noticing the presence of older women or designing programs based on our perceptions of their needs; it requires that we begin with older women's own assessments of their pastoral needs. Widening the circle requires that we enter into genuine dialogue with the older women in our congregations. Dialogue might take many forms and could include engaging in a process of vocational discernment at key points of transition in later life, such as retirement or relocation to a new residence. Through this process we might assist women in determining the shape of discipleship at such points as an expression of the moral praxis of aging. Dialogue includes listening, as well as speaking, and might lead to other ways to hear women's life stories. For example, a congregation might record both the lives of older women and the history of the congregation by gathering the stories of longtime members, in either written or oral form.

Widening the circle to become a community of gracious inclusion requires us to recognize the heterogeneity and diversity among older women. We cannot assume that the needs or desires of older women are identical. Older women represent a broad age range covering at least thirty years, from sixty-five to ninety-five. Older women represent diverse ethnic groups, educational backgrounds, and occupational experience. Each woman's life is unique. One of the ways in which we dismiss a person is to overlook her individuality and think of her only as part of a group. To dismiss the unique features of a person's life is an element in the process of cultural imperialism through which persons are designated as Other.

A vision of the church as an ever-widening circle of gracious inclusion is an expression not only of inclusiveness but of deeply held theological convictions about the nature and purpose of the church. The church does not come into existence primarily through human effort but is called into being through God's gracious activity. As such, a sharing in the life and love of the triune God marks the community of faith.

An Ecclesiology of Koinonia

Foundational to a vision of the church as a widening circle of gracious inclusion is an ecclesiology of koinonia, in which relationship or communion between God and God's people defines the nature and purpose of the church. This approach to ecclesiology, which has been articulated in different variations by Orthodox, Roman Catholic, Protestant, feminist, and liberation theologians, has also become increasingly central to ecumenical dialogue about the nature and purpose of the church.[22]

A theology of koinonia views the church as "a web of interwoven relationships" in which "love, acceptance, forgiveness, commitment, and intimacy constitute the church's very fabric."[23] Koinonia, or communion ecclesiology, is thoroughly Trinitarian, characterizing Christian community as a sharing in the "life and love of the three persons in one God."[24] This approach stresses love as the core of the Christian revelation that is generated through the intimate connection of the three Persons of the Trinity. The attributes of personal being and interconnectedness that characterize the Trinity are central to this understanding of the church.

An ecclesiology of koinonia focuses on relationships not only among the persons of the Trinity but also among human beings and God, among the members of the communion of saints, among members of a particular community of faith, among church communities, and among the various bodies within the larger Christian community.[25] The divine love, expressed in the love shared between Jesus and the disciples, is the foundation of the church. The character of this divine love is such that the church cannot remain turned inward, but is called to spread the divine love within and beyond the Christian community.

Communion ecclesiology challenges the notion that "the individual is the basic unit of human reality and that all types of community are secondary and accidental."[26] The Trinity, understood as a community of Persons, serves as the corrective image to this distortion by asserting that the relations among the Persons are central to the nature of God. In this view of the Trinity, "God's relationality and God's oneness are mutually interdependent; neither has priority over the other."[27] Individuality, however, does not disappear into some communal identity. Individuality "remains crucial and basic, but not more basic than community."[28] The two are held in tandem. Human beings created in the image of God are similarly constituted as persons through relationship. The church is also understood to exist both as "a community and as a group of distinct persons."[29]

Common to various formulations of communion ecclesiology are three central commitments. First, koinonia emphasizes spiritual fellowship or communion between human beings and God rather than the institutional aspects of church. An intersubjective ontology is implicit in this approach to ecclesiology. This vision of the church is grounded in a relational view of the Trinity as Persons in communion; this relationship is constitutive of what it means to be a person. Within this understanding of community, the dynamic relationship between individuality and communal identity is highlighted. Implicit in communion ecclesiology is the relational anthropology we have already discussed; it preserves the dynamic interplay between individuality and connection. Second, the need for both unity and diversity in the church is recognized and encouraged. Third, in feminist and liberationist expressions of koinonia a commitment to mutuality in community organization and authority structures is fundamental. This commitment to mutuality requires monitoring structures of power and authority and thus reflects the assumption that social context is not neutral.

Articulating a vision of the church and identifying the ecclesiology that can sustain such a vision is our first step. However, we must remember that our vision of the church is not just about what is; it is an eschatological vision. Churches will embody koinonia or become widening circles of grace to varying extents. In order for this vision to become a reality, we must examine the model and practices of care that embody this vision.[30]

From Vision to Care

To promote the flourishing of older women, we need not only a vision of the church but also a way to live out this vision. I propose the way of gracious inclusion as the context in which to name the theory and practices of care that enable congregations to live out this vision of the church. Such an approach to care is theologically and ecclesially grounded, takes the social context into account, is informed by clinical insight, and is expressed through specific ecclesial practices.[31] Five basic assumptions (mentioned in chapter 1) inform this approach to care:

1. Human beings are created in and for relationship.
2. The church community is best understood in terms of a koinonia or communion, and this shared common life is marked by mutuality and reciprocity.
3. Human development is a relational process occurring within a social context.
4. The social context is not neutral, but requires critique.
5. Context, difference, and diversity are valued. These assumptions determine an approach to care that is expressed through specific practices.

Practicing Gracious Inclusion

A vision of the church makes little difference unless this vision becomes a reality in some way. Through Christian practices, or how we actually do things, we live out our vision of the church. Our vision of the church always has an eschatological dimension; we get closer to living out this vision some days more than others. Through practices we attend to the gap between our vision and the reality of our lives. Christian practices require a sense of awareness of our human limitation and sinfulness, and they call us to repentance when the distance between our vision and our way of being becomes too great.

Practices can be defined in various ways. One approach to practices is reflected in Rebecca Chopp's understanding of them as culturally shaped "patterns of meaning and action" that come to life in individual instances.[32] Another understanding of practices finds expression in the writing of Dorothy Bass and Craig Dykstra, who focus primarily on Christian practices as "things Christian people do over time to address fundamental human needs in response to and in light of God's active presence for the life of the world."[33] What both definitions share is the conviction that practices embody our beliefs about and understandings of the world. Because I am focusing on ecclesial practices here, my approach reflects that of Bass and Dykstra: I understand Christian practices to be shaped not only by social forces but also by the Divine-human relationship through which we are constituted as persons. Through Christian practices, in which we live out our convictions and commitments, we respond to God's grace.

At times, our social practices conflict with our Christian practices. For example, social practices that assign women to limited roles in late life or stereotype them as either grandmothers or mean old women conflict with the gospel's calls to recognize our common humanity and our unity in Christ (Gal. 3:28). In such instances the professed faith and the practices within the community of faith fail to match. Such a conflict between the narrative of our faith and our practice of it occurs when we profess that hospitality is central to our understanding of community, but we discourage the homeless man from coming back to the service next week. When we engage in practices uncritically, we are unaware of the mismatch between the faith we profess and the faith we live. Through critical reflection on Christian practices we become aware of this mismatch between intention and reality. Such an awareness can lead to the reform of current practices and the identification of practices through which we can live out our vision of gracious inclusion.

I propose three practices specific to the care of older women and designed to deconstruct their cultural invisibility. These practices are grounded in a vision of the church as a community of gracious inclusion, but they extend beyond the congregation into the larger community. Practices of *tending relationships* affirm the social, relational, and communal dimensions of aging. Through these practices we care for the primary relationships in which older women experience aging and communities that support those women. Through the practice of *narrativity* we deconstruct the power of cultural imperialism and its attendant stereotypes of older women. This practice allows older women to author, at least partially, their own late life stories. The practice of narrativity also challenges binary thinking and encourages the embrace of ambiguity and paradox. Through the practice of *prophetic witness* we advocate social policies and programs that address systemic issues of injustice. We also affirm narratives of resistance through which older women define themselves and reject constricting definitions. By juxtaposing a theological vision of aging with cultural images and practices, we challenge the temptation to reject aging as a part of our human finitude and embrace our creaturely, embodied, temporal existence.

Although the three practices are interconnected, narrativity precedes relational and prophetic practices in some respects and weaves itself through them. We interpret the important relationships of our lives through narrative frames. For example, if our experience has shaped us so that we interpret the world as a hostile place, this lens will alter our actions in relationships, including our willingness to trust others or be vulnerable in relationships. Relationships shape our identity, and narratives describe this sense of self. The communities to which we belong, including the church, also have narratives, and these can move us to prophetic witness as an expression of our sense of corporate responsibility. Although we distinguish the practices for heuristic purposes, they are inseparable and interwoven in our lived experience.

These practices express both pastoral and congregational care. Some require advanced training and may be most appropriately practiced by persons with skills in pastoral care and counseling, such as a layperson with professional skills or a pastor with skills and gifts in care and counseling. Others are congregational expressions of care, and the responsibility for them falls on all members of the community of faith. To follow the way of gracious inclusion, we must encourage these practices when they are present in communities of faith, institute them where they are not, and dismantle counterpractices that oppress older women.

Narrative Practices of Care

We construct our lives, our sense of self, and our view of our place in the world through the stories we tell about the world and ourselves. Through narrative we construct a life story and a sense of self. We compose these stories not in isolation but in dialogue with the stories others tell about us. Personal, family, communal, and cultural narratives all intertwine and form our identity.

Personal narratives communicate our internal experience of ourselves and may include our bodily experiences, our self-perceptions, and our dreams and hopes for the future. Yet these personal narratives are formed not in isolation but in the context of family life. Family narratives, which relate our sense of belonging and place in a particular family, also influence personal narratives.[34] For example, Katherine's sense of self includes the narrative of being adopted by her aunt at a young age because her mother, ill and dying, could not care for her. To her aunt, who was unable to bear her own children, Katherine was a gift, a special child. This narrative gave her a sense of esteem despite the early loss of her mother. Cultural narratives often communicate the dominant meanings of the larger society. Cultural narratives about African American women influence Katherine's own personal narrative. At any point, a number of counternarratives can challenge the dominant view. By telling Katherine that she was special, her aunt challenged dehumanizing cultural images of African American women.

Communal narratives are composed of stories of belonging to a particular community. As an adult, Katherine chose a community of faith that reflected her understanding of herself at that point in her life. Although she was raised in an African American Baptist community, she now finds the style of worship and theology no longer fit her self-understanding. She has chosen a racially mixed congregation in which to live out her desire to bridge differences among people.

These various forms of narratives often intertwine. Communal narratives influence our personal narratives, and we may interpret communal narrative through our personal stories. What happens when these various narratives clash? At times, the stories we tell about ourselves don't fit the stories our families, communities, and cultures tell about us. As we saw in our opening narratives, some older women feel deeply this conflict between their self-understanding and the cultural or communal narratives.

This mismatch of narratives can raise self-doubt and confusion because many older women personalize this conflict and assume responsibility for it. Some women resolve the conflict by revising their self-narratives rather than by challenging the construction of communal and cultural narratives that threaten to overwhelm them. This narrative conflict invites pastoral care through narrative revision in which women reclaim their own voice and agency. To describe this revisioning, Rebecca Chopp employs the term *narrativity,* which she defines as "the active agency of writing one's own life."[35]

The practice of narrativity identifies conflicting narratives and encourages older women to claim responsibility for their life stories while recognizing the relational and cultural contexts in which these stories unfold. By helping women claim agency to interpret their experience rather than submit to cultural definitions, narrativity supports interplay between autonomy and connection. A pastor or friend can encourage an older woman to reinterpret problematic life stories through formal pastoral counseling with a skilled pastoral therapist, through an exploration of vocation with a pastor or spiritual director, or through informal reminiscence with a lay caregiver. For example, Sarah grew up believing that motherhood should be her primary role, yet she found her most satisfying sense of identity through her teaching career. She carries a sense of failing to fit the expectations of her generation, but a revision of narrative might help her accept herself and her life choices. Through pastoral conversation, women facing life transitions such as retirement or widowhood may also learn to fashion hopeful future stories.

Narrative practices also require a congregation to examine the stories it tells about itself and its members. How does the church with the logo on its bulletin "A Place for Everyone" handle the homeless woman who wanders down the center aisle during worship or the developmentally disabled adult who answers the preacher's rhetorical questions out loud? Do these narratives foster gracious inclusion, or do cultural narratives crowd out theologically grounded perspectives? The practice of narrativity leads us to prophetic witness. It teaches us the mutability of cultural meanings. It impels us to bear witness to meanings of human life and aging that arise out of the Christian tradition and to offer a countercultural witness to narratives that diminish older women.

The Practice of Tending Relationships and Caring for Communities

Through the practices of tending relationships and caring for communities, we nurture the interpersonal, family, and communal connections that form the context of older women's lives. Tending relationships includes acknowledging and supporting family, marriage and committed partnerships, and friendships. This is a corporate responsibility that calls congregations to create an ethos of connection and interdependence in tension with the individualism of American culture. Laity and clergy alike create such an ethos. Clergy can set an expectation that care is the responsibility of the entire congregation and not the clergy alone. Laity can ask one another, and older women in particular, about their relationships with children, spouses, friends, and siblings. It is often easier to give care than receive it, but the willingness to receive care, whether by accepting a casserole after a hospital stay or sharing one's life with others, affirms our interdependence.

Tending relationships includes clinically identified practices, such as pastoral counseling of individuals and families, through which relational conflicts may be healed, and support provided in the face of loss and grief. Such practices require knowledge of human development and relationships, and those who have counseling skills and knowledge are often most effective.

Caring for communities involves attending to the quality of communal life, which includes encouraging interplay between individual and communal identity and spirituality. Such interplay can prevent an exaggerated individualism or an oppressive communal homogeneity that suppresses individuality. In such communities, diversity is valued and nurtured.

Another dimension of communities that support older women is hospitality, which is about welcoming others, and creating a space for those who may be different from us in age, physical ability, or ethnicity, or who simply do not share our interests or point of view. Hospitality is essential when older women enter communities for the first time. For example, Katherine found a congregation that welcomed her and her gifts when she moved to a new community following retirement. As an important dimension of gracious inclusion, hospitality recognizes our interdependence and reminds us that we never make it on our own.[36]

To care for communities may require forming support groups for older women. Many such groups exist in local churches in the form of women's Sunday school classes, societies, task forces, and programs. Other churches lack such groups or fail to link older women to them effectively. (We will see some examples of this in the next chapter.) Programming often fails to meet the needs of older women. Sarah does not enjoy the potlucks for the senior members of her church. She longs for programs that engage her intellectually and challenge her to grow. The most common programming for older adults, however, is this "meet and eat" variety, usually accompanied by entertainment or light program.[37] Katherine involves herself in ministry to a refugee family because it lets her work with people of all ages and it stretches her to encounter a culture different from her own. She prefers intergenerational activities to those designed exclusively for older adults.

The Practice of Prophetic Witness

Prophetic practices challenge social attitudes and policies that are oppressive to older women. Advocacy for public policy can be an expression of prophetic witness, especially when it recognizes that the cultural construction of age and gender raises issues of economic security, caregiving, and abuse. Older women are more likely than older men to struggle with these concerns, which often reflect lifelong patterns of gender discrimination.

As in Julie's congregation, advocacy can take the form of intervention at the individual level, including assisting older women, for example, who are faced with economic difficulty, the burdens of caregiving, or violence. Because women in such situations are vulnerable, it is often appropriate for a trained caregiver to make an assessment and an initial intervention. Intervention, however, is only one dimension of advocacy.

Advocacy includes speaking on behalf of older women and pursuing concrete action on their behalf. On an individual level this might include bringing attention to domestic violence, which affects women of all ages, and providing referral to a shelter attentive to the needs of older women. At a larger social level, advocacy can mean challenging systemic oppression and promoting public policies that support older women. This means, for example, examining employment practices and such public assistance programs as Social Security and Medicaid, because a significant percentage of the recipients are older women.

Narrative practices and prophetic practices intersect. One point of connection is through the recognition and support of women's narratives of resistance. Katherine, for example, refused to be defined as a cookie-baking grandma. She sees herself rather as a bridge builder, and she engages in bridge-building activities. A second point of intersection is to juxtapose our cultural narratives with the Christian narrative as a way to challenge harmful cultural assumptions. For example, a discovery that our practices of selecting leaders in the church overlook older women will call for a revision of our practices.

Prophetic witness points toward a theologically grounded view of aging. It encourages us to embrace our finitude rather than distancing ourselves from our elders, whom we perceive to be on the border of life and death. To accept our own finitude is to recognize that we all live on this same border; we dwell together in this region.

Narrating life stories, tending relationships, creating communities, and bearing prophetic witness are the concrete ways in which we live out a vision of the church as a widening circle of gracious inclusion. Through these practices, the church embodies a theologically grounded view of aging and promotes the flourishing of older women. In the following chapters, we will examine each of these practices through the stories that older women offered in their interviews.

CHAPTER 4

Narrative Practices of Care

The interviewer gives the invitation, "Tell me a little bit about yourself." But where does one begin to tell the tale of a life? The point at which one begins, or the story one chooses, often reveals a theme central to one's identity. Joan begins the story of her life with her conversion at the age of six.

> Well, as I think about my life, all my life has been based on Christian belief. I have a lot of faith, since I was six, when I had my first real Christian conversion experience. I was in school, a little country school and our church was nearby. They were holding a revival service and that minister preached to the children. Then he gave an altar call and a lot us went down to the altar—we were sitting on the front row. My experience was very emotional. My grandmother came up to me afterwards—my mother was not there, she was at home with her other children—and said: "Well go on home and tell your mother that you are saved." And so that is what I did.

Joan emphasizes the presence of God and the role of faith in sustaining her throughout her life. Following the account of her conversion, she moves immediately to the story of her mother's death and describes the way in which prayer delivered her from grief. For Joan, the church as a place of belonging and support has played an important role in her life story and has shaped her identity as a woman of faith.

Joan does not simply begin her story with birth and move chronologically through time. She chooses which stories to tell and places them in a particular sequence, thus constructing a narrative through which she tells us something about who she is, how she defines herself, and how she makes sense of life. Joan's conversion story is an important part of her larger narrative, in which her identity as a Christian is central and her faith is the means through which she has overcome difficulties.

Constructing Meaning and Identity

Through the stories we tell and the narratives we weave from these stories we make sense out of life. Narrative theory articulates how stories function to construct meaning and our sense of self. Implicit in narrative theory is the assumption that our interpretations of reality are socially constructed. Because we construct this reality through the stories we tell, narrative serves as an organizing structure of human life. David Polkinghorne defines narrative as a meaning-making device through which individual components are organized into a coherent whole.[1] Through narrative we construct meaning in our individual lives and build frameworks of interpretation through which we view the world. Through personal, familial, communal, and cultural stories we organize and maintain our interpretations of the world. Narrative is central to our human existence.[2]

Sometimes, however, the stories we tell or that others tell about us diminish rather than empower us. Sometimes our personal narratives conflict with the narratives of our families or communities. Narrative practices of care, the primary focus of this chapter, provide the means through which problematic stories can be challenged and conflicting narratives resolved. Storytelling as an expression of care provides an appropriate and sustaining interpretation of our stories and life narratives.[3]

To understand how narrative practices can address problematic or conflicting stories, we need first to discover how story and narrative function. We will then turn to the various forms of narratives through which we construct our identity and worldview. After a further description of narrative practices, we will tell stories of four women to illumine the intersection of personal, communal, and cultural narratives in the transition of retirement.[4] Sarah's story illustrates what occurs when communal and personal narratives about retirement conflict. Rose's experience clarifies the process of revising a self-narrative following a retirement, and Ann and Elizabeth's story exemplifies the positive consequences of narratives cohering. These stories allow us to imagine how pastoral care can enable life-affirming narratives.

Forms of Narrative

Stories, as Herbert Anderson and Edward Foley have observed, are "privileged and imaginative acts of self-interpretation."[5] Stories are not an objective reporting of events; they are interpretations of events from our perspective. The stories we choose to tell and those that remain unspoken reveal our perceptions of ourselves. We not only tell stories of our own lives, but our family and our culture tell stories about us and to us as well.

Although we often think of *story* and *narrative* as interchangeable terms, in narrative theory they have distinct meanings. Individual stories describe an incident, an event, or a point in time. Narratives are larger interpretive frameworks and may be constructed from full-blown stories, as well as from short accounts occurring in conversation or interviews.[6] As we weave these stories and fragments together, they create a narrative, or "web of stories," through which we construct our sense of self, define meaning in our lives, and communicate these meanings to others.[7]

Our sense of self emerges from multiple story strands and varying forms of narrative. We can understand the overarching narrative of self-identity, the "me" we describe to others, as composed of interlocking narratives. These include narratives of subjective self, intersubjective (relational) narratives, narratives of the perceived self, and communal narratives. These forms of narrative shape our identity and allow us to communicate our multidimensional experience of being a person.[8] Without suggesting a complete theory of personality, this description illumines the way narratives function in forming our sense of self and the world.[9]

Personal or Self-Narratives

Personal narratives communicate the beliefs we hold about ourselves. These narratives are not exclusively our own creation but are formed in the context of our relationships with others. In this sense, personal narratives always have an interpersonal dimension, because to a large extent we see ourselves through each other's eyes. We tell stories about ourselves and to the significant people in our lives. We don't, however, always tell the same story the same way. For example, we might tell the story of a night on the town quite differently to our college roommate than to our mother or father. The fact that we tell different versions of the same story to different listeners illustrates the importance of the relational context to our sense of self.

Our narratives of the subjective self are often communicated when we utter first-person constructions such as "I think," "I feel," or "I believe." They include the point of view from which we perceive and act upon the world. This dimension of subjective narrative is evident in Joan's story of her conversion. By beginning her life story with this event, she tells us that this is a defining moment in her life. Her identity as a Christian, a person of faith, is central to her self-identity.

Our subjective narrative also includes an experience of embodiment, or our sense of what it means to live in our particular physical body. This narrative includes how we see, value, care for, or reject our physical selves and how we experience ourselves in our bodies. Mary, age eighty-four, illustrates this sense of embodiment by referring to her changing appearance. "I look in the mirror and I see the wrinkles and I see the baggy eyes. I know I am older. I think a little older, yet at times I think as young as I ever did." Mary is aware of the physical changes accompanying age, and her experience of embodiment is a dimension of her self-identity.

Subjective narratives include what we might call our self-concept, or our understanding of our abilities, skills, or capacities. They can include dimensions of the self that we do not we routinely present to the world. For example, Ann, age seventy, has developed an interest in woodworking since the age of sixty, and she has learned to use a number of power tools. Her self-concept includes this new competency in woodworking, something not immediately evident to others.

The Perceived Self

The perceived self influences our self-narratives. Narratives of the perceived self include the stories others tell about us and reflect the way others see us. At times, others' perceptions may reflect cultural stereotypes or assumptions and fail to fit our own self-concept. My initial perception of Ann was that she fit the stereotypical image of a white-haired sweet little old lady, but she is quite comfortable operating a chainsaw or table saw. Her self-perception includes these competencies, but my initial perception of her, influenced by cultural age and gender assumptions, did not.

Intersubjective Narratives

Narratives of our relational or intersubjective self are in some ways inseparable from our subjective narratives, if we assume that our subjective sense of self is always formed in relationship with significant others in our lives. Intersubjective narratives may also include our internalization of the perceived self. If I describe myself as friendly, optimistic, and outgoing, it may be because other significant persons in my world affirmed in me these behaviors and affects.[10] Narratives of our relational self include our understanding of self in relationship to others and the roles by which we define ourselves, such as daughter, mother, sister, and friend. Rose, for example, discovered after her husband's retirement how much her sense of self had been shaped by the role of "preacher's wife." The retirement provided freedom from this role and an opportunity for a revised self-definition.

Communal Narratives

Just as interpersonal relationships shape us, so do the communities to which we belong. Communal narratives convey what it means to be a member of a community and our place in it. The larger Christian narrative, the life stories of its members, the history of the congregation, and its context shape the narratives of Christian communities or congregations. As the body of Christ, the church comes into being through God's gracious activity and signifies God's continuing presence in the world. Part of the continuing task of the larger church is to proclaim and witness to the interconnection of the Divine and human narratives. Congregations strive to be faithful to the vision of gracious inclusion as they live out the Christian story through their narrative in a specific time and place.

Just as the subjective narratives of an individual convey a sense of identity, congregational narratives communicate the identity and purpose of a community. Westview Baptist Church, for example, chose to remain in the city in a racially changing neighborhood when other predominantly European American churches were moving to the suburbs.[11] This decision did not come easily and followed a long process of deliberation by the congregation. One consequence of this decision was that many members left. Those who stayed adopted the phrase "We are not here by chance" to communicate the church's revised sense of self-understanding that emerged from their decision to stay in the community.

A community also has an understanding of how its members and groups relate to each other. Westview's decisions impacted not only its subjective narrative of identity but also the relational narratives of its members. This church chose to be in relationship with people in their larger community. This resulted in some conflict within the congregation, which was resolved only over time and through a prolonged dialogue, and yet this dialogue precipitated a narrative of Westview as a place that welcomes all people. This relational narrative has expanded so that the community now welcomes persons regardless of sexual orientation and continues to explore what it means to be an inclusive congregation.

Narratives of the perceived community also inform Westview's identity. Though its subjective and relational narratives are largely consistent with the way others perceived it as a progressive and welcoming community, such external perceptions do not always fit a community's self-perception. Those who know nothing of Westview's story may assume that because it is a Baptist, and formerly Southern Baptist, church, it would not invite into membership persons of varying sexual orientation. This is hardly Westview's understanding of itself. Westview describes itself as an open and inclusive church even in the statement of mission hanging in its sanctuary.

Temporality and Narratives

Stories are shaped by the perspective of the storyteller and by the time frame in which the story is told. Stories tell tales of the past, describe the present, and help us imagine the future. Westview's identity includes its past and present practices, both of which will shape its future. Andrew Lester has noted that we often pay more attention to the past and present dimensions of story in pastoral care and counseling than to the future dimension.[12] Yet developing hopeful "future stories," he argues, is an essential task of pastoral care because the absence of a hopeful future story promotes despair.[13]

These future stories often operate outside our awareness, but we do notice when they fail us. Julie, for example, had imagined a long life with her second husband, but her future story changed dramatically when her husband died, for she lost not only her companion but also her home. It appears that she is still revising her future story, trying to find one that can sustain her in the midst of the unexpected changes. Julie's faith and her connection with her church have provided some basis for hope as an unanticipated future unfolds.

Assisting in the creation of a hopeful future story is an important dimension of the narrative practice of care with older women. This takes on a particular urgency in the context of meaning often assigned to old age in Western culture. When aging is defined primarily as decline or loss, it is all too easy to assume that an older woman should live primarily in the past or present. After all, how much future does she have? But the future dimension of our lives can take on profound significance in the midst of life transitions, such as retirement. How we envision the future can lead to disappointment when this future does not materialize, but it can also increase the chances of realizing a future filled with rich meanings.

Snippets of stories, episodes of key events, tales we tell, and stories that our friends, families, and communities tell about us wind through past, present, and future to become the narratives of our lives. In the best circumstances, these strands weave themselves into a whole that provides a sense of identity and helps us to make sense of our lives, by being liberating and life-affirming, by helping us face difficult events and find a way to move forward. But sometimes our stories constrict and confine us, keeping us trapped in self-defeating interpretations. At such times, we may not realize that our view of our life is one interpretation and that others are possible. At this point, pastoral intervention as narrative practice can make a positive difference.

Addressing Problem and Mismatched Narratives

Narrativity, as a practice, is an interpretive process through which we review and revise the stories of our lives. As a practice of care, narrativity is a collaborative endeavor between the storyteller and the care provider, who work together to create life-sustaining narratives, identify inconsistencies in stories, and find alternative interpretations. Through attentive listening, caregivers can assist older women in challenging and reinterpreting problematic and conflicting narratives and composing alternatives that increase a sense of agency and well-being. Through this process of "authoring" our lives, we have some degree of choice about the interpretive frameworks through which we construct meaning and identity.

This view of narrativity draws significantly on the narrative therapy theories of Michael White, David Epston, and others.[14] White and Epston propose that the meaning attributed to events, rather than some internal psychological structure or dysfunction, determines behavior.[15] They read a family's patterns of interaction as a behavioral text that can be interpreted in the therapeutic process.[16] They suggest that persons seek help when their lived experiences contradict or conflict with the dominant narratives of their lives.

Narrative practices of pastoral care and narrative therapy share a common goal: the generation or identification of alternative stories that allow new meanings and possibilities for action.[17] Although pastoral caregivers may not be engaged in therapy, we can use techniques of narrative therapy, such as revising stories and identifying alternative stories, as part of the general practice of pastoral care in church settings. Pastoral caregivers should also note, however, problematic stories or narrative conflicts that are so complex as to exceed their skills of reinterpretation and that may require the intervention of a therapist.

Problem narratives are interpretive frames that cause distress and reinforce self-defeating beliefs or behaviors. When an interpretive lens takes hold, we ignore stories and experiences that could challenge it. Julie, whom we met in chapter 2, feels ashamed of her financial difficulties and her dependence on the church. Her interpretation of the situation keeps her somewhat isolated from the other residents in her community in order to protect her secret. If Julie shared her secret with others, she would likely discover that she is not the only older woman to need assistance or face poverty following widowhood.

Through deconstructive listening, the caregiver can help Julie separate herself from the situation. Rather than seeing herself as a dependent and needy person, she might come to recognize that her current difficulties are the consequences of lifelong patterns of gender discrimination that placed her at an economic disadvantage as she became older. Although this might not affect her finances, which are a real concern, it could change her interpretation of herself. Through story reconstruction, she might identify alternative story strands that have been obscured by the problem story. For instance, she might discover the benefit of interdependence and value the contributions she has made to her family and community over the years. She might come to understand the assistance she receives as an expression of appreciation for these contributions and an affirmation of her worth as a person aside from her economic value. This revised interpretation might also allow her to explore additional sources of support, such as Supplemental Social Security income, that she might have chosen to do without because of feelings of shame regarding her financial needs. Change occurs through externalizing the problem, the collaborative process of narrative deconstruction, and reinterpretation of the problem.

A *narrative mismatch* occurs when the stories that others tell about us do not fit with the stories we tell about ourselves. Conflicts may occur among the narratives with which we construct a sense of self and our world. Such a clash often occurs for older women. A critical social analysis can help identify conflicting narratives. To challenge the problematic cultural constructions of age, we need to recognize them. Once the narrative conflict is identified, a woman can decide to resolve it by privileging one narrative or living creatively in the conflict.

The practice of narrativity requires attention to negative cultural constructions of age and the way these shape the narratives of women and their communities. Many of the women we interviewed articulated images of aging that reflect cultural norms from which they immediately distanced themselves. To some extent these women were aware of the mismatch between their personal narratives of aging and the widespread cultural images.

Some women develop strategies to resist destructive cultural perceptions of aging and to try to live creatively in the gaps between mismatched narratives. For example, Ann (from chapter 1) is very aware that older women become less visible with age, but she has developed strategies to create a self-narrative of someone worth noticing. Despite the cultural pressure to disappear, she has learned to juggle, which gives her visibility in a crowd. Ann and Elizabeth reflected on how juggling allows Ann to resist invisibility.

Ann: I don't let people make me invisible if I don't want to be. I'll do something silly, you know.

Elizabeth: If we go to a shopping center, I never know for sure whether Ann is going to have a couple or three juggling balls in her pocket or not. She doesn't like to shop. I like to go in every shop and look. But if she gets bored, I might look over there and she is in the corner juggling and there is a crowd around her.

Ann: Of course, once you start juggling, somebody's going to come up and say, do you know how to do this? Jugglers find each other. It is one of the best skills I guess that I have ever learned…Well, when you see a seventy-year-old woman start juggling, she's not invisible anymore.

Ann has chosen a creative resolution of the mismatch between a belittling cultural narrative and her own narrative of being creative and vital.

Mismatched Narratives

We return now to Sarah's story, first introduced in chapter 2, as an example of mismatched narratives. Sarah looked to retirement as a time to be more active in her church, but her church seemed to view retirement as a time of disengagement.

Sarah: Edged Out

Sarah is a seventy-three-year-old European American woman of average height with just a touch of gray in her brunette hair. Dressed in blue slacks and a yellow top, she has just finished a day of substitute teaching and is articulate and professional in her manner during the interview. She and her husband of fifty-three years have a large family of five children and thirteen grandchildren. Sarah had what she describes as conflicting desires to be a stay-at-home mom, "which was the thing to do after WWII," and to be a teacher. These two desires "worked at cross purposes" for a while in her life. After relocating to the city where they now live, with all her children in school, Sarah completed a master's degree in education. Her area of expertise was working with behavior-disordered children in middle school.

At this stage of her life, Sarah finds that she does not feel much different from twenty years ago. She says that her politics are the same and that she still has a liberal take on religion. She and her husband have faced health restrictions in the last three years, which has made her more aware of her age and less active than others of her age with no health restrictions.

Sarah retired at sixty-two, at the same time as her husband "because it seemed like a good idea for both of us to retire at the same time." She soon discovered that she "had less hobby potential" than her husband and found herself substitute teaching several days a week. One of the surprises for Sarah was the response of her church to her retirement. She states that within a six-month period from sixty-two to sixty-two-and-a-half she aged ten years in other people's eyes. She had been active in leadership positions in the church, but when she retired "they just programmed me and put me over here."

In Sarah's narrative of her anticipated retirement, travel and shared adventures with her husband would fill her time. Her husband, however, faced some unexpected health challenges after retirement that made travel difficult. Sarah did not expect that retirement would be difficult, but when her vision of the future changed, she needed to find a new way of being retired. Travel was not an option, and she discovered she did not have much "hobby potential." She turned to her church, her primary area of volunteer activity in the past, imagining that this would be a good place to use her gifts of leadership and discover a renewed sense of vocation.

Unfortunately, a narrative mismatch occurred between Sarah and her church around expectations and images of retirees. Sarah was surprised and angered by her experience of "aging ten years in six months" in the eyes of others. Although she still saw herself as competent, she felt that members of her congregation stereotyped her and saw her as less competent than she had been. Sarah noted that the church often had asked her to take leadership positions when she was in her fifties. After her retirement, these offers dwindled. She said that she and others in the church were "stereotyped right up that stair step." She experienced retirement as stigmatizing her in the eyes of younger church leaders. As a consequence, she felt she had to prove her competency to the younger leaders.

I think they just hear the word retirement and they guess your age because they know the age of your children and so forth. They just categorize you. And you have to re-prove yourself, as if you were a student in class, that I am capable of doing so and so...Somehow, now that you are retired [it is assumed] it's because you are not as sharp or capable as you once were. You are not working. There are certain assumptions [made]. We look old, and I'm afraid we're locked together in a lot of respects, unless we can push the boundaries so that we really set up a relationship with younger women.

Sarah saw a change in the perceptions and behavior of others toward her after she retired. She described a board meeting in which she experienced this change of attitude.

At cabinet and board meetings, after I retired, I began to feel I was treated differently. You've been in a meeting where someone talks too much, you know, they get a certain reaction. I would get that feeling on a simple answer or a simple question—we have to humor her and we'll move on. It is more in the tone of voice. But it didn't happen just once. It's definitely a change in the way you're perceived.

She resisted being pigeonholed as "retired" by volunteering for things before being asked, which she had not done previously. Before her retirement, she felt that the church often asked her to take on a leadership role. Afterward, she had to be more proactive.

And I had to fight against it. My point is—in that I didn't wait to be asked a lot of things. I met it head on by volunteering for things that I thought, "they're big things." We're not allowed in the church to do anything big. But there are certain things that either engage you or keep you interested, or there aren't. I could feel that. I did feel that this was definitely true of the larger church...Men are more ready to help you across the street when you don't need help than they are to see you as a person who perhaps has done as good a job as they did. And I don't know whether this is chivalry, you know...for them or what exactly. But it was kind of funny.

Clearly the church is and has been an important part of Sarah's life, despite her anger and surprise at her congregation's response to her. She still wants to be a part of this church and to contribute to this community. "I think the church gives a place of belonging, though, and it's very, very important to some people, even when we are no longer able to attend."

Sarah did not expect her self-narrative to change so much with retirement. Unfortunately, Sarah did not find the church's communal narratives of retirement or the perceptions of her by others as a retired person as positive or consistent with her own sense of self. The church reinforced the cultural narratives of retirement as a time of disengagement and diminishing competence. As a consequence, Sarah is now less active in her congregation than she was. Finding herself edged out of leadership positions in the church, she has gone back to work as a substitute teacher. Although some days are difficult because of her health limitations, she feels that the school sees her as competent and appreciates what she has to offer.

Narrative Practice and Mismatched Narratives

In this situation, the church reflected cultural biases and stereotypical images of retired persons, and it exemplified these communal narratives in its practices of leadership and recruitment. Because such narratives damaged Sarah, the church is losing a competent volunteer who cares about the church and wants to be engaged in its ministries. As long as this narrative goes unchallenged, the members of the congregation will probably attribute Sarah's reduced activity to her retirement rather than to their reaction to retirement. As long as this perception continues and the church communicates a lack of interest in its retirees, the congregation may find that other retired members will lose interest in the church. A narrative approach to pastoral care could help the church identify the assumptions about retirement implicit in its practices of leadership recruitment.

Sarah did not identify her experience as a narrative mismatch, but she knew that she saw herself differently than the way leaders in her church saw her. She suggests that a conversation with the pastor or other lay leaders would have provided an opportunity for vocational discernment.

> I mean, I think they might have sat about ten of us down at that time and said, "how do you see your role? You contributed a lot. Do you want to continue? Do you want to do something different?" I think they make a mistake. You've worked for thirty years and you are burned out with whatever you've done for thirty years. And the churches, it seems to me, still pigeonhole you. If you've been a teacher, you might

have to be on the education committee. I might like something else, you know? I don't think they [the church] do enough in that respect. And I think someone needs to sit down and help you.

Had such a conversation taken place, Sarah might have found other ways to negotiate the mismatch of narratives.

Sarah invites us to see retirement as a time of transition and discernment rather than disengagement. Pastors and lay leaders who recruit and equip members for leadership can learn to negotiate such narrative mismatches. Sarah does not suggest that the pastor alone might have provided such guidance. Narrative practice in this instance might occur through attentive listening that would allow both Sarah and the caregiver to discern the implicit narrative of retirement in Sarah's story and in the congregation's practices.

If we take seriously a theological vision of aging as a time of spiritual growth, retirement provides an important opportunity to reassess one's vocation as a Christian. Such vocational discernment happens best in community and requires a congregation to accept willingly the gifts and service of its retired members. Approached this way, retirement lets one discover new avenues of service to the church as an expression of one's lifelong commitment to discipleship— a profound gift to both the individual and the church.

Revising a Self-Narrative: Balancing Continuity and Change

Sarah's story reminds us that retirement is an important life transition. For Rose, it provided new freedom from old roles and an opportunity to revise her self-narrative. Rose's story illustrates how older women can simultaneously revise a life story and maintain a continuity of narrative that sustains them in the face of changes.

Rose: New Freedom

Rose is a petite and energetic seventy-year-old woman of European descent. Married for forty-six years, she has two adult children and three grandchildren. Neatly dressed in a brightly colored, tailored pantsuit, she graciously invites the interviewer into her well-appointed living room. Rose grew up in the south, in a middle- to upper-middle-class home. Her father was a general practice physician in the days when doctors still made house calls. As a result, she identifies her mother as the "more present parent"; though her father was loving when he was home, "we just didn't see that much of him."

Following graduation from high school in 1947, Rose attended college. Trained as an elementary school teacher, she taught for three years before marrying, and she continued to teach until the birth of her first child. Although she has worked on and off throughout her life, her career was set aside while she was raising children. Her husband's career as a Lutheran minister took precedence and often determined where they would live. This mobile life was a big change for her, having grown up in the same town and living in the same house all her life prior to her marriage. When her husband retired, she selected the city in which they retired. She chose a city in which they had lived previously and where her adult children now reside. She has old friends, including high school friends, in the community.

Some of the activities that are important to her now are her work with the church's homeless shelter, involvement with her grandchildren, learning new computer skills, e-mailing friends, reconnecting with old friends, and investing in her marriage.

An intelligent and self-reflective woman, Rose thoughtfully articulates the positive dimensions and complexities of this stage of her life. The years since her husband's retirement have been a time of discovery and growth for Rose, both in terms of her own self-identity and in her marriage.

Aging is not the primary category through which Rose identifies herself, yet she is not unaware of her age. Rose enjoys good health and acknowledges that her health contributes to her current sense of life satisfaction, though she is aware that this may change as she ages. Reminders of her age often come from her interactions with other persons who are younger. A recent incident made her aware that "older women are really sort of past noticing somehow."

One of Rose's discoveries following her husband's retirement was the extent to which her identity came from her husband's position and her role as the "preacher's wife." After retirement, she discovered the extent to which her self-narrative depended on others' expectations, the "perceived self," and communal narratives about "the preacher's wife." Rose shares her reflections on this discovery with the interviewer.

Interviewer: Tell me a little bit about what your life is like at this point. Do you have any particular challenges or surprises as you've reached this age?

Rose: No, no, not terribly. I think mine may be a little bit different from some people that you talked to in that we were so involved in the church and had such good friends there. The preacher and the preacher's wife roles, kind of, but at that time I wasn't really that aware that I was in a role. But since I'm out of it, I realize that I was.

And so part of the big change of being retired, of Jim being retired, is getting out of the roles, which has had mainly good sides, but it also has added to the invisibility.

I realized that in Marble Hill I had an identity as the preacher's wife. I wasn't really particularly aware of it at that time, but have realized since that that gave me a visibility and an influence sometimes that I don't have just on my own. And that has made me stop and think, oh, maybe I wasn't as strong a person as I thought I was then, and maybe it was just the role that was helping me have some of the influence that I thought I had.

Interviewer: But you became aware that some of your role was, in a sense, derivative from his and that's something you've thought about or struggled with?

Rose: And I was not all that aware of it then. I just thought since then that that was part of the way other people saw me.

The influence of interpersonal and communal narratives on Rose's subjective sense of self is illustrated in this conversation. Jim's retirement allowed Rose to recognize how she had allowed the expectations of others to shape her life story. Even though she had a career and identity as teacher and mother, others often related to her merely as the "preacher's wife." Although this role provided a certain standing and easy entry into new communities, it was also constraining. Retirement and the move to a new community allowed her to define herself in new ways in this new phase of her life. Although Rose has enjoyed the changes, she also notes that loss of her role added to her invisibility as an older woman. Overall, Rose has discovered new interests and new dimensions of herself, reconnecting with old friends and shaping a new relationship with the church. She continues to be an active volunteer in the church, free now to choose the activities that interest her.

This is not the first time Rose has faced changes. Because of her husband's career, she has moved many times and adjusted to several new places, including France. She is not unaware of the effects of such changes, but she attributes them not primarily to age but to other life events, including their recent move.

Interviewer: Is your life different now than it was ten years ago?

Rose: Oh, my, yes. I don't know that it's really so much related to my age as it is to a lot of other things, to retirement, moving away from where we had had both social and professional responsibilities.

Oh, yes. Our life is much more spontaneous, less scheduled. Not only did we move away from professional responsibilities, we moved away from social responsibilities. And we had not lived here since 1977. And while we had sort of kept up with some friends, their lives had moved on and so had ours. So we don't have a circle of friends that we picked back up with. So we don't have any social obligations, really. We don't owe them a dinner or anything like that. It builds up, you know, if you lived in the same place all those years. So that's been nice. We've liked that.

On the other hand, I do miss my friends because… I quit teaching when we moved to Marble Hill and I had time there to make friends. And I had really good close friends, and many of them–of many different ages. And I miss that. That's not something you can do when you're this old, is make all those friends unless you're in a situation like we were in where you are thrown into all these different situations.

Rose can enumerate the changes, but she still sees herself much as she did when she was younger. This balance is evident in her reflections on the change and continuity.

Interviewer: Do you feel like you're essentially the same person you were twenty years ago, or is there balance between some of the continuity in yourself and the growth and change in yourself?

Rose: I think there's a pretty good balance. Yes, I'm the same person. But I have more self-confidence and I'm a broader person. I think I've continued to broaden.

Interviewer: So growth, in a sense, is a fuller development of who you've been.

Rose: I think so. Yeah, yeah. I still have some of the same quirks I've had all these years

How might we understand this balance of change and continuity in Rose's life, and how might this inform pastoral care with other older women? One useful perspective is what has come to be called continuity theory. Developed by Robert Atchley, continuity theory describes aging as a continuous process of development and adaptation occurring over the life span.[18] This theory provides a way to understand Rose's experience and provides a model of adult development in late life.

Balancing Continuity and Change

Continuity theory asserts that "continuity and change are themes that exist simultaneously in people's lives."[19] Developed out of more than twenty years of research and longitudinal studies of midlife and older adults, continuity theory provides a way to understand how older adults adapt to change through continued learning across the life span. Many older adults show considerable consistency over time in many dimensions of their lives, including self-concept, interests, and living arrangements, despite significant changes.[20] A key principle in the theory is the understanding of continuity not as the absence of change but rather "as the persistence of general patterns" over time.[21] The theory does not suggest a homeostatic state but rather an ability to be flexible and to adapt to the future in light of past and present views of the self. Most people's lives reflect the coexistence of change and continuity. From this perspective, the goal of adult development is not a state of static equilibrium but adaptive change.

Continuity theory, like narrative theory, is constructionist. It assumes that people develop constructs that make sense of what is occurring in the world and why.[22] Both theories focus on the mental frameworks or narratives that allow people to adapt to life circumstances and maintain a sense of well-being. Continuity theory, like narrative theory, views persons as engaged in the construction of a life story, weaving together various strands of subjective, intersubjective, communal, and cultural narratives. By making choices over time, people construct a sense of self that both adapts to change and maintains consistency in changing circumstance. Because continuity theorists assume that people are constructing a sense of self, the individual's perception of continuity is more important than any objective determination.

Continuity theory helps us understand how Rose can see herself as essentially the same now as twenty years ago, while acknowledging changes in her life. She is not unrealistic and does not hold a static sense of herself. She has continued to adapt and revise her self-narrative while maintaining a sense of continuity with the past. Continuity theory argues that maintaining a continuous sense of self over time is not the result of inflexibility and resistance to change but the consequence of constant adaptation and revision of a life narrative. This image of older adults as flexible and adaptable contradicts a stereotype of older women as resistant to change and incapable of learning.

Narrative Practice and the Revision of Self-Narratives

Life changes require adaptation and may call for narrative revision. Pastoral care as narrative practice can assist in this process. Some narrative conflicts may cause severe distress and require therapeutic intervention in revising narratives, but in many cases this is not required. Simply encouraging an older woman to tell the story of a significant transition may lead to the discovery of new insights or interpretation of events. Sometimes referred to as life review, this process of storytelling often occurs naturally in older adults. The difficulty in facilitating this process may lie with younger listeners who understand it as living in the past. Both narrative and continuity theories argue that it is through telling a tale that we can revise it. The very act of storytelling is interpretive; it helps us adapt to change while maintaining continuity of the self over time.

Life review can be informal and may occur spontaneously in pastoral visits, or it can be formalized. The interview process provided a structured opportunity for life review, and many of the participants commented that they had said things they had not intended to say or had come to new insights through this process. Although Rose revised her life narrative largely on her own, she observed that the interview nevertheless gave her new insights.

Congregations can encourage life review and narrative revision. For example, a youth group might embark on an oral history project and gather the recollections of older women in the congregation. Older women might be invited to participate in an autobiography project as a part of an adult education program. Life review can also be a part of the ministry to homebound members and would provide visitors with a structure for their visits. In some cases, lay caregivers might discover significant distress and the need for in-depth pastoral counseling. In these cases, they can and should call for pastoral supervision and referral resources.

When Narratives Cohere

Some narratives conflict or need revision, but others cohere and provide support for women in later life. Ann and her partner Elizabeth discovered how the mutually supportive narratives of their lives, their relationship, and their church community helped them enter creatively into retirement and a new community. The practice of narrativity can assist in this process of cohering narratives by helping individuals and communities identify those story strands that affirm late life as a time of spiritual growth and moral praxis.

Ann and Elizabeth: Women in the Woods

Ann is a vibrant and active seventy-year-old European American woman. She and Elizabeth, her partner of eleven years (also European American), are both retired and very active in their community, serving as mentors for troubled teenagers. Following their retirements, which occurred at about the same time but at different ages for each, they sold their home in the city and moved to their country home, renovating their cabin for full-time residency. They found that though they could live comfortably in one property, they could not keep both.

Ann, formerly a psychotherapist, has two grown daughters and one ten-year-old grandson. Appearing for the interview in a bright pink shirt and blue pants, Ann's reflections about her life are filled with humor and animation. Ann is quite active in her local Unitarian Church and felt she has finally "come home" after being somewhat dissatisfied with other Protestant churches of which she was a part. Ann's sense of humor is reflected in her comment that she and Elizabeth have a "heavy metal relationship," a reference to the power tools Elizabeth has given her to pursue her woodworking hobby. Ann also stresses that to age gracefully one needs to eat healthily, remain active both physically and mentally, maintain a network of support through friends and family, and have a positive attitude, all of which she and Elizabeth strive to do.

Elizabeth, sixty-five, is more introverted and communicates a quiet strength. Wearing a dark plaid shirt and pants, she appears unassuming and calm. Elizabeth took early retirement due to degenerative arthritis, which has improved since her retirement. She states that her job was "literally becoming a pain in the neck." Elizabeth states that her involvements since retirement have been more political and that she is an active environmentalist. She is proud to have been elected as a member of the county board of health, a volunteer position, as a relative newcomer to the rural county in which she resides. She feels that some of the expertise she brought from her work is being utilized in this position. As a part of this position, Elizabeth has become interested in the water quality in the streams in their area. She has recently become qualified to test water samples.

Elizabeth is also aware of her invisibility as an older woman and comments on this but deals with it differently than Ann. A seminary graduate and participant in advanced clinical pastoral education, Elizabeth is sensitive to the needs of both elderly and dying patients and their families. Like Ann, Elizabeth is independent and hopes to live that way as long as possible. Elizabeth stresses the need for others to find value in aging individuals and the need to share human touch with the elderly.

Ann and Elizabeth agreed to be interviewed together, but I will focus on Ann's experience of retirement because she discussed it in more detail than Elizabeth.

Ann agreed to retire at age sixty-eight in order to join her partner in relocating to the cabin they owned in the country, a significant distance from her job. She retired somewhat reluctantly, fearing she would have no reason to get up in the morning.

> I wasn't ready to retire. Let's see, I was sixty-eight? sixty-nine? sixty-eight, I guess, and still felt pretty vigorous. And I was actually scared to retire. I was afraid I wouldn't have a reason to get up in the morning—that nobody would care if I came or went. I wouldn't have that sense of purpose about my life.

Ann's personal narrative of retirement included the discovery that it did not fit her preconceived notions of it, which were derived from the cultural stereotypes. For Ann, retirement became a time to discover new abilities and interests, deepen her relationship with her partner, and find a new church community that supported her in the midst of change. She volunteers in a middle-school mentoring project, the Meals on Wheels program, and in her Unitarian congregation. New interests since retirement, such as woodworking, have been an important part of her life.

What gave Ann a reason to get up in the morning? How did she move beyond her fear that retirement would consist of empty, boring days? First, her personal narrative included other experiences of adapting to change. As a result, she felt she had internal resources that allowed her to interpret retirement as a positive experience. Second, Ann had the support of her partner, and their relational narrative also contributed to a positive transition. Her decision to retire came partly from her partner's need to retire and their desire to keep their country property. Ann is also in relatively good health, and she and her partner have enough income to live frugally but comfortably.

A significant factor that Ann mentions repeatedly is the support of her church community. Whatever its communal narrative about retirement, it offered Ann a supportive place to reinvent herself.

> And now I've discovered the Unitarian faith, shall we call it, which has the kind of liberalism and freedom and dignity that just really resonates for me. I'm looking more at spirituality in more of a—what do I want to say—an independent sense, because, as I said, I grew up and spent most of my life in conventional churches where we were taught dogma. Now, I feel like I've come home. Yes, and to have all the freedom that I need and have wanted all my life. To explore without

having a set of beliefs thrust on me is a wonderful feeling. And now that I'm retired–the best thing since menopause– I have the time to do more of what I feel comfortable doing and that I feel rewarded for doing. It's gratifying to be able to choose where I put my energies. I'm busier than I ever thought I would be as a retiree. Beyond being involved with the church in the renovation classes, I also sing in the choir. I'm co-chair of the publicity committee. I'm in the Sunday morning services committee. There are a number of things like that that have kept me busy in this church community.

Ann's church community has fostered her intellectual and spiritual growth. It has provided a sense of freedom to define herself in new ways through her various volunteer activities and her new interests. It offers an intergenerational community in which age does not seem significant. She observes that she is the youngest member of her Sunday school class. Involvement in this community has allowed Ann to interpret retirement as a time of continued self-discovery and growth. Even though she expected to be disengaged and discarded, her church helped her find a new vision of what life could be. It has supported Ann in discovering an alternative narrative of retirement.

Narrative Practices of Coherence

Ann was fortunate. She was able to resist cultural expectations through the revision of her self-narrative and the supporting narratives of her primary relationship and of her community of faith. How can we create such conditions for the older women in our congregations? First, we can examine our assumptions about aging and older women. We can assist congregations to discern limiting or negative perceptions of aging that may be reflected in congregational practices. As we saw in Sarah's experience, such congregational attitudes are often not consciously expressed but emerge through other practices of ministry, such as leadership recruitment. By identifying these implicit negative narratives, we can attend to the ways we can revise them.

Other congregational practices that bear examination include the ways in which older adults are portrayed in sermon illustrations or educational materials. We can also examine the programming for older adults. Do the programs provide opportunities for growth and development, or do they assume that older adults are not interested in or capable of learning? We can provide pastoral care at times of life transition and develop appropriate rituals for these transitions, such as retirement or moving from one's longtime home to a retirement residence or assisted care facility. In all these ways, congregations can help older women enrich and deepen their lives.

Narrative practice of care can also help older women identify negative images of aging that have shaped their life stories. As evident in Ann's story, women can internalize limiting images of aging. Through life review and attentive listening, pastoral care providers can help older women transcend these culturally bound stories and tell alternative stories of resistance that allow self-continuity. The primary purpose of the narrative practice of care with older women is to identify and deconstruct narratives that limit or demean. At the same time, our task is to help create narratives, both personal and communal, that affirm the abilities, contributions, and lives of older women. We can find ways to help women construct hopeful future stories even in the face of life transition and loss. Such life-affirming narratives will allow older women to embrace aging as a time of growth as well as change.

Only through careful listening can we identify problematic stories, note narrative mismatches, and locate alternative interpretations that are healing and life affirming. When we asked the older women interviewed what advice they would give to younger pastoral care providers, the answer was unanimous: listen. Katherine, whom we met in the last chapter, puts it this way:

> I'd tell them to listen closely. To listen. To take time to listen and take the time to perceive these older women as being as worthy as their moms and grandmoms. And through listening they can get some clues as to how they can draw from this important resource to meet needs. I see listening as the pastor's biggest challenge and their greatest charge.

For narratives to cohere, women must find supportive relationships and communities that recognize and affirm their gifts. Narrative practices of care intertwine with the practices of tending relationships and creating communities. All these practices recognize the relational context in which older women live out their lives. Where supportive communities do not exist for older women, we work to create them. We now turn to these relational contexts and practices of care.

CHAPTER 5

Tending Relationships
Single Women in Late Life

Just as Kate's fingers move along the yarn and the needles and create a whole garment from a single strand, so she has carefully knit together a network of family and friends who have supported her as a lifelong single woman who is visually impaired. Now, at age seventy-two, she lives alone for the first time since losing her eyesight in midlife and tries to maintain the independence that has been an important part of her self-narrative. Yet Kate's carefully crafted network of family and friends is beginning to unravel.

Like Kate, we all live our lives in the context of family, friendships, and other important relationships. We shape and are shaped by the relational context of our lives; we are persons-in-relation, despite our illusions of autonomy.[1] Much energy goes into caring for these relationships, and many of the stories we tell are about healing, improving, leaving, or losing these connections. Our interpretations of our relational experiences become a part of the large narratives of our lives.

Relational practices of care, to which we now turn, intertwine with narrative practices. Through the practices of tending relationships and caring for communities we affirm and nurture the interpersonal, family, and communal relationships central to the lives of older women. Before we can explore relational practices of care, we must first have a clear picture of older women's networks of family, friends, and communities. In this chapter, through the words and stories of Kate, Katherine, and Joan we explore some of the contours, complexities, and unique dimensions of the lives and relationships of older single women. Such narrative portraits help us move beyond our stereotypical assumptions about older women in general by introducing us to the lives of particular women. Through a pastoral assessment of each woman's narrative in dialogue with gerontological research, we identify some of the opportunities and challenges facing older women that might be addressed through relational practices of care.

Older Women's Relationships

Kate's story reminds us of the central role that kinship and friendship ties play for older women.[2] Repeatedly, studies have linked well-being in older women to both formal and informal support networks, which include extended family, friends, and organizations such as churches and senior centers.[3] Many feminist theologians employ this image of a network or web to illustrate the relational character of women's lives, finding this a more appropriate portrayal of women's development and maturation than autonomy.[4] Although some feminist theorists hold that the relational character of woman's lives is essential to women's nature and others argue that this is a product of the social construction of gender, the centrality of relationality to the majority of women is not contested.[5]

Older women, like all human beings, find themselves in a complex variety of relationships and relational roles. Because women are wives, mothers, sisters, daughters, friends, partners, lovers, grandmothers, aunts, mentors, teachers, and so forth we might use various frameworks to understand these diverse relationships. I have chosen to organize these reflections on women's experience through the categories of kinship ties, marriage and partnership, and friendship. In this chapter we will hear the stories of some of the significant relationships, particularly those of family, and will explore the contours of the lives of older women who are currently defined as single. In the next chapter we will turn to narratives of marriage and partnership.

Single Women

An older woman is defined as single in the gerontological and sociological literature if she lives alone and does not have an intimate partner. It is important to note that single does not mean singular, in the sense of existing apart from others. As the stories in the pages ahead demonstrate, even single women are located in a complex network of family relationships and friendship networks. These relational contexts provide social support and a sense of identity and purpose for many older women.

Single women include lifelong singles and widowed and divorced women. More than half of women over sixty-five are single: 45 percent are widowed, 8 percent are divorced, and 4 percent have never been married. Significantly, older women more often live alone than do men (42 percent compared with 20 percent), and this too has repercussions for their well-being.[6] But not all women living alone have the same issues. Although widowed and divorced women are considered single, it might make more sense to consider them as formerly married, because the life course and one's sense of self is shaped by marriage in a way that is different than if one does not marry.[7] Yet marriage is still considered the norm in U.S. society, and terms such as *old maid* or *spinster,* used to describe women who remain single, reflect this bias. Even the term *never married* suggests marriage is the normative state. Being ever single is still a stigmatized state in our society.[8]

Through the stories of Kate, Katherine, and Joan we will recognize some of the similarities and differences between ever-single, widowed, and divorced women. We also must remember that although such categorization helps us organize our experience, each life is unique and good pastoral care attends to the distinct features of each situation.

Ever-Single Women

We return now to Kate, an ever-single woman who also provides a glimpse of how one older woman deals with disability.[9]

Kate: Finding Her Way

Standing on the front porch, I try to remember the doorbell sequence to let Kate know that someone familiar is at the front door. Although not exact, the rhythm of the rings sounds enough like the cadence of "Candy Man," a reminder of Kate's salesman father, to bring her to the door. Kate, seventy-two, has been visually impaired for the last forty years, having lost her sight at age thirty-two. Now living alone in a busy, urban area, she relies on the doorbell signal to discern between friends and strangers.

Being single presented a challenge when Kate initially lost her eyesight. She returned home to live with her widowed mother, Iris, where she has remained for the last thirty years, and to take advantages of opportunities for job retraining available in a bigger city. She continued to teach for some time, shifting from the public schools to working with visually impaired children.

Kate has managed to maintain a high degree of independence, which is very important to her, though she now finds this more of a challenge since Iris's death. Although Kate did most of the shopping and cooking, Iris provided companionship and did small tasks like sorting the mail. Although Iris was somewhat frail and did not venture out much in her later years, she was in relatively good health until her death at home at age ninety-seven. Other extended family members, who once lived nearby and offered Kate support and practical help, have either relocated or are busy with jobs and growing families. The neighborhood church Kate belonged to most of her life, which was also an important part of her network of support, has closed. She has begun attending another church nearby but knows fewer people there and finds it hard to make a place for herself.

Kate notes that her friends are aging at different rates, and some are less willing to "get out and go" than she is. Kate now spends much of her time tending the house, keeping up with friends, and pursuing her hobbies of pottery, gardening, and teaching knitting at a nearby senior's center.

DISCUSSION. Kate is among the 4 to 5 percent of ever-single older women, and like the majority of these women, she lives in an urban area.[10] Kate is also in good health, as is true for many older ever-single women, who tend to be healthier than widowed or divorced women as a group.[11] Ever-single women also tend to report higher levels of life satisfaction among single older women. Several factors may contribute to these higher levels of life satisfaction; for example, unlike divorced and widowed women, ever-single women are not adjusting to the loss of a life partner. Ever-single women have also had time to settle into a single life and establish networks of support and patterns of meaningful activity. As a group, ever-single women have a more positive outlook on life.[12] This positive outlook might affect their assessment of life satisfaction.

Kate, like many ever-single women, is college educated and was focused on her career for many years. Ever-single older women tend to be more highly educated and more likely to have had careers than married or previously married women, which can result in greater economic security for ever-single women.[13] Ever-single women who have had to support themselves financially may have higher incomes than widowed or divorced women, receive higher pension benefits, and are less likely to fall below the poverty line than other single women.[14]

Family, for ever-single women, may be broadly defined and include parents, siblings, and extended family members, such as nieces and nephews. The care of older family members, particularly parents, often falls to ever-single women who do not have the responsibility of spouses and children. This was true for Kate, who lived with and helped care for her mother until her mother's death. In addition to a close parent-child relationship, sibling support is often very important to ever-single women.[15] Siblings may provide both emotional support and practical help. So, for example, for many years, Kate's older sister lived next door to Kate and her mother. Although Kate's sister moved away about ten years ago, due to her husband's job, she still visits every three to four months to assist Kate with large shopping trips and other household tasks, as she did when living next door.

Older women may also consider friends as part of their family network. Friends who are particularly close may be considered "fictive-kin."[16] Because many ever-single women have less practical help from family members than do married or previously married women with adult children, close friends become increasingly important and are counted on for key support when other family members are no longer present.[17] Friendship has certainly been an important part of Kate's life. Some of her current friends are from church; others she met initially while working, still others are neighbors, and some share her interests in pottery and gardening. These friendship ties may be more determinative of Kate's well-being, and that of other ever-single women, than kinship ties.[18]

PASTORAL ASSESSMENT. I have often watched Kate use her hands to guide herself along as she cooks, finding the right pot or pan, the right knife, or feeling for bad spots in the tomatoes. Now that she is living alone for the first time since she lost her eyesight, she is also feeling her way along as she seeks to maintain her independence. Routines established in the past few years, particularly as her mother became more frail, assist in this process. She walks to the corner store for basic items such as bread and milk and is able to maintain her house with some part-time help. Family members still assist with home maintenance and big shopping trips.

Kate's sense of independence emerged early in her life. After finishing college, Kate moved to another part of the state where she taught elementary school for a number of years. Fighting a losing battle with diminishing eyesight, she returned home to live with her mother and to be near other family members only when it became clear that she would lose her sight completely. She knew their support would be important in the transition. Following her relocation, she sought retraining at an Institute for the Blind near her home and continued to teach elementary children at the Institute. It is important to Kate to learn new skills in order to maintain as much independence as possible.

Kate's efforts to maintain her independence are balanced by her attention to the creation of a broad network of support. Although family members who lived nearby provided support in the past, Kate also engages in a number of activities to maintain this network. She is active in a local congregation, travels twice a week by bus to a pottery class, and teaches knitting at the senior services center nearby. She also makes good use of the telephone and Braille typewriter to keep in touch with family and friends. Freed from the responsibility of caring for her mother, Kate now spends more time away from the house pursuing her hobbies and visiting with friends, but she misses her mother's companionship.

One of the changes in Kate's life is a shrinking of the web or network of family and friends that has been an important source of support for her as an ever-single woman. She is actively engaged in widening her support system as she searches for a new church and increases her involvement in activities that put her in contact with other people. Although a number of women face loss of social support in later life, it has particular consequences for Kate because of her visual impairment. Kate's adjustment to the loss of her sight was eased by the retention of visual memories from being previously sighted and by the support of a close family. Since her mother's death, Kate has experienced her disability as having a more limiting effect on her life than it did previously.

For the last thirty-five years, Kate has been surrounded by people she knew well. Now her mother has died, her sister no longer lives next door, and her nephew who lives nearby travels frequently with his work and is busy caring for a young family and thus visits her less often. Kate notes that her friends who used to come visit "are getting old and don't get out as much." Many of her friends have moved away from the inner city and find negotiating the distance and traffic daunting. Kate is now living alone for the first time since she returned home to live with her mother.

In addition to her family, the church has always been an important part of Kate's life and a source of support to her. Kate grew up in her neighborhood church and remained there for many years. Like Kate, many of the members had their favorite pew, which meant she could easily find people she knew, even with impaired sight. She knew that George would be in the fourth row down on the left, and that Margaret always sat in the middle of the back row. At about the same time that Kate's support network of family and friends began to contract, her home church closed because of dwindling membership and a changing neighborhood. Although Kate can walk to another church of the same denomination nearby, she has not found a home there. In her new church she does not know where people are, even though she knows some of the members, nor can she find her way to them because it is so big. Reflecting on this experience, she says, "It is not pleasant to be isolated in a place where you know people."

As Kate was describing her difficulty in finding a new church home, she told me that she had not made a good adjustment to being blind. She said, "Even though I have been blind for thirty-five years, I only now realized that blindness is a social impediment." I asked her what had led her to this conclusion, and she observed that her experience of isolation in the familiar setting of the church has contributed to this assessment.

Kate is aware that her world changed with the death of her mother, but she attributes the changes and problems more to her "poor adjustment to being blind." Kate's narrative of her church experience is in many ways consistent with Kate's sense of self. Her independence is important to her, and she has always had a sense of being responsible for what life brings. In her current situation, however, this narrative of personal responsibility may not be helpful.

Kate does not seem to hold others accountable for their perceptions that render her invisible. She tends to excuse those in her new church who make little effort to greet her or integrate her into the new congregation. She does not, for example, hold the church or the church members of her new church responsible for welcoming her more effectively. She says she would rather go to a large church that is harder for her to reach, but where she can be comfortably anonymous, than be isolated in a familiar place. It is not that Kate is any more warmly greeted in the larger church, but the expectation of anonymity makes her invisibility easier to bear.

Just as Kate cannot see where familiar faces are in her new church, I wonder to what extent others see and notice her presence, an older disabled woman. Some congregations simply do better than others in welcoming and integrating newcomers. However, unless this church is simply an unfriendly place to all visitors, its lack of welcome of Kate may be due to an implicit communal narrative influenced by negative social attitudes toward aging unconsciously expressed in the communal life and practices of this community.

It is difficult to determine if the congregation is able to perceive Kate's needs at this stage of her life. She describes this congregation as mostly composed of families with young children or middle-aged members and notes that there are few other members her age. Her fellow Sunday school class members are focused on issues of family life and childrearing, which are not her concerns. Kate does know a few people in her new church, and perhaps there is a presumption by other members that she does not need to be integrated any further. Because Kate is private and independent, few may know that she now lives alone and yearns for new needs to be met, such as a need for company. Although Kate has a relationship with the pastor and enjoys her dedication and energy, it is not clear that the pastor is aware of Kate's current situation or her possible needs for pastoral care.

Just as Kate has learned to pick up dropped stitches in her knitting, she is trying to pick up the stitches of her life that have slipped through her fingers. As her networks of support have contracted, she has made efforts to expand them so that she can maintain the independent life she has created for herself. It is unfortunate that her church community has not been a significant resource for her in this process.

Relational Practices with Ever-Single Women

Through the interconnected practices of tending relationships and creating communities, the church embodies a vision of gracious inclusion and challenges the individualism of our culture and church. Individualism leads us to value independence over dependence and leaves little room for interdependence as central to human existence. A vision of the church as a community of gracious inclusion affirms our interdependence as relational beings, created in the image of a relational God.

The individualism so pervasive in our culture is evident in Kate's own narrative and in her relationship with her church. Kate has seen herself as independent all her life, and to a large extent this is true in the sense that she has managed quite well as a single woman. We define independence as autonomy and the ability to take care of oneself, but in fact all of us are deeply embedded in webs of relationships that make our perceived independence possible. Kate's life has been significantly intertwined with others, and this interdependence has made it possible for her to manage "on her own." As long as Kate continues to view herself as only independent, she may expect herself to manage without help from the church and not hold the church responsible for its failure of hospitality. If the folks in the church think only in terms of independence, they may conclude that Kate is doing fine on her own and that they have no responsibility for her. Here we see how narrative and relational practices of care intertwine. For the church to tend to the important relationships in Kate's life and for Kate to receive this tending, both need to revise their narratives to accommodate interdependence as a central category.

Part of the practice of tending relationships with single women is being aware of the contours of relational networks in which women live their lives. Tending requires attending: paying attention to these networks of family, friends, and communities. One of the ways that churches can attend to this important dimension of women's lives is to conduct an inventory of significant relationships. This does not have to be a formal process but can occur in informal conversation– for example, as new members join the church. We do this almost automatically for persons with families; we notice how many parents or children are in a family. We tend to see single adults, however, as singular rather than immersed in a relational network of extended family and friends. Single persons still have families and are embedded in networks of relationships, whether or not they have life partners or children of their own. As previously noted, friendships often are quite important to older women and may comprise a "family of choice," which provides both the practical and emotional support families normally supply.

A second dimension of tending relationships with single women is being attentive to relational losses. This means not only providing support through a period of grieving but helping a woman expand her circle of support when losses are experienced. Kate has lost her mother and friends, and other family members are less available than they once were. It is not clear whether Kate's new pastor is aware of the death of her mother. In Kate's case, an attentive pastor might simply inquire about Kate's family and friendship networks. Following the death of her mother, a follow-up visit sometime after the funeral might include inquiring as to how the church might be supportive of Kate as she adjusts to this loss in her familiar network.

The new congregation Kate is attending has not yet become a community of support for her. One might argue that the primary purpose of a congregation is worship and service, rather than meeting the needs of its parishioners. Yet a vision of the church as a community of gracious inclusion affirms the relational dimension of our lives as a reflection of being created in God's image. Thus, helping Kate become integrated into the life of this community and facilitating her involvement in worship and service is central to the community's identity. It may also be that as Kate becomes a part of the community, she will discover resources that strengthen her networks of support.

As we saw in chapter 3, the practice of creating community has much in common with the practice of hospitality. A simple way for the church to extend hospitality to Kate and to move toward being a gracious community for her would be finding one or two persons who would be willing to be worship partners for her. Such a ministry might include meeting her at the door of the sanctuary, helping her learn the layout of the new sanctuary, introducing her to people, and helping her know where people generally can be found in the congregation. This orientation to the congregation would both help integrate Kate into the congregation and help folks in the congregations come to know Kate as a unique individual, not us as "the blind woman in the back row." Such a ministry does not require significant pastoral skill, and could be easily undertaken by lay members of a committee responsible for evangelism and new member incorporation. Hospitality is central to being a community of gracious inclusion, but it is a practice often overlooked or undervalued in congregations.

Kate has experienced the church as a community of support in the past and turns to it as a place of belonging. Through being attentive to the relationships that have sustained Kate and engaging in the practice of intentional hospitality, the church and this particular congregation can become a place of gracious inclusion for Kate.

Supporting older women who experience the loss of a close relationship late in life is an important part of the church's ministry. Loss of a significant relationship is a fairly common occurrence in late life. Loss of a spouse or life partner and the transition from wife to widow are part of the life journey of many older women. Next we will meet Joan and through her story will explore a transition faced by a number of women–that of widowhood. Because Joan's husband was ill for several years before his death, her story also raises issues of women as caregivers.

Widowed Women

Sitting in a prominent place on the coffee table are the devotional books that Joan and her husband read together daily. These books remind Joan not only of her husband but of her lifelong Christian faith, which sustains her as she makes the transition from wife to widow. Joan's experience of widowhood is uniquely her own, yet it is an experience shared by many older women. Married women are increasingly likely to face widowhood as they age: 45 percent of women over age sixty-five are widowed, 55 percent of women age seventy-five to eighty-four are widowed, and 79 percent of women over the age of eighty-four are widowed.[19] These demographic realities confirm the observation that widowhood is a woman's issue.

Joan: Sustained by Faith

As she sits in a blue recliner, Joan, eighty-three, is relaxed and ready to reminisce about her life. Joan shares that her deep faith has helped her get through difficult times in her life. Two months after moving into a retirement community near her former home, Joan's husband of fifty-eight years died from complications due to pneumonia after a long period of declining health. A widow for six months at the time of the interview, Joan credits her family, friends, faith, and many prayers for helping her to cope with her new life. Her extended family of four children, five grandchildren, and three great-grandchildren are an important source of support, as are her church and her network of friends.

Born and raised in South Carolina, faith and education were important to Joan and her family. She attended college, where she met and married her husband in 1941. During the childrearing years, her husband's job required significant travel. Now that she is adjusting to life on her own, she appreciates the independence she developed during that period of her life.

Joan attended church every week with her family. At the age of six, influenced by a close relationship with her United Methodist grandparents, Joan converted to Methodism and has remained an active member since. As a dedicated member of the church, Joan continued to play the piano for her church until moving into the retirement home. Occasionally she can still be found singing in the choir of her home church during holidays.

During the interview, since Joan had been widowed for only about six months, tears still came easily to her eyes. She reflected on the reminders of her husband's absence, such as particular parts of her daily routine and seeing the devotional books they used to read together.

> Well, I've had days when I've missed him so much, you know. You can almost feel his presence sometimes. And he had certain little habits that were…well, he was a man of habit. He was a night person. I was a morning person. I got up earlier than he; he never went to bed with me—that is, after he became ill. He would put the earphones into the TV. And he would look at TV or read or something after I had gone to bed. He slept a lot during the day, too. But, I would get up and have my little quiet time, devotional and so on, and then go and fix my breakfast, and then he would get up about that time. And he always walked right over and picked up

his Bible and *Upper Room* and came and sat with me and we had our devotional in the *Upper Room*. Well, I tell you those first mornings [shakes head], it was just so hard because he wasn't here. There are just several things that he would do that caused me to remember him. And I do have very, very fond memories, wonderful memories.

DISCUSSION. The death of one's spouse or partner is one of the most disruptive life events that older women face.[20] It involves multiple losses—the loss of the status of being married, loss of a clearly defined role as wife, and often loss in income, personal identity, and social status, as well as the loss of companionship, friendship, love, and emotional and intellectual support. At the same time, widowhood is an expected life transition for many older women. As noted earlier, it is a transition that increases substantially with age, with nearly eight out of ten women over eighty-four having lost a spouse.[21]

It is clear from Joan's narrative that the first few months were the most difficult. Joan's experience is consistent with research indicating that depression is more common in the first few months of bereavement and generally decreases after a few months to levels similar to depression of nonbereaved persons.[22] Although widowhood can also have a significant impact on the physical and mental health of widows in the first months following death, these effects diminish significantly over time.

The experience of widowhood is different for each woman. Several factors shape the experience, such as levels of dependency and interdependency in the marriage, circumstances surrounding the death, economic impact of the death, availability of social supports, and whether the death was considered timely or premature.[23] The death of an older spouse is generally considered "on time"—that is, fitting a socially accepted timetable—whereas death of a younger spouse or a child is "off time," upsetting the expected life cycle. Joan seems to have experienced the death of her husband as "on time." This is probably due to the mitigating factors of his age (eighty-five) and his illness prior to his death.

As a European American, middle-class woman, Joan had access to resources that eased her transition to widowhood. Class and ethnicity are additional mediating factors influencing the adjustment to widowhood. Research conducted in the 1970s by Helena Lopata, one of the first researchers to explore widowhood, found that working-class women initially experienced less disorganization in their lives following the death of a spouse than women from other socioeconomic groups.[24] Over the long term, however, middle- and upper-class women may make a better adjustment to widowhood, primarily in terms of social integration and financial security. Presumably, this is a consequence of the availability of greater resources to these women because of their socioeconomic status. Many women experience a drop in income following a husband's death, but this is typically greater for those with lower levels of income to begin with and few additional financial reserves. Living arrangements following widowhood are different for various ethnic groups. Both black and white women were more likely to live alone following the death of a spouse than Hispanic and Asian widows, who were more likely to live with other family members.[25]

The circumstances surrounding a death also influence the course of grief. Joan would likely have experienced some anticipatory grief as her husband's illness progressed. In some ways, Joan experienced the loss of her husband as her familiar partner through his increasing dependency, which changed the dynamics of their relationship.

> Before he died he had a lot of heath problems—and still looked healthy. But, he became so dependent on me, even though he didn't look sick, because he had diabetes, he had neuropathy, he was beginning to get neuropathy, he had heart problems, high blood pressure, and beginning signs of Alzheimer's.

The death of Joan's husband meant the loss of a lifelong partner, yet it also meant release from the burden of caregiving. Joan's grief includes a complexity of feelings generated by these two realities.

> We always told each other that we loved each other, and that was the last thing we would say before going to bed. But I look back and I just think he was so irritable part of the time after he got so sick, depressed, and then at times he was so sweet. But I just—you look back and you don't realize what you missed until it is already gone sometimes…But I'm sure that we were as close and we—we were just human. We were normal.

Although Joan does not explicitly express relief, it is clear that the years of caregiving have taken a toll on her. In a subsequent interview, she reports some stress-related health problems she experienced prior to her husband's death. In situations like Joan's, in which illness precedes death, it is not uncommon for widows to experience a sense of relief from the release of the caregiving burden and from the end to the spouse's suffering. Yet these very same feelings of relief sometimes cause feelings of guilt. Pastoral caregivers assist widows in the transition to widowhood by interpreting this complex of feelings, the strange mix of sadness and relief, as a normal part of grieving.

PASTORAL ASSESSMENT. Joan has coped with the loss of her husband by drawing on a number of internal and external resources. These internal resources include positive memories of her marriage, her faith, her previous experiences with death, and her own inner sense of resiliency. Joan's first experience of death was the death of a younger sister at the age of two, followed by her mother's early death. Her older brother died at fifty-two, and a second younger sister died eight years ago. As she reflects on a conversation in which she and her friend were discussing the deaths of the friend's sister and of Joan's little sister, her attitude toward grief emerges.

> The other day I was talking with a friend of mine. Her little sister is sick and she was talking to me (about how upset she was) because she wasn't taking care of herself. I said: "But don't forget to tell her you love her." My little sister is deceased. And we both just started crying. And she said: "I didn't realize it had been so recent that your little sister died. I said: "Yes, eight years ago." I mean—you know that place never gets filled. You just learn to live around it.

Like many older women of her generation, Joan finds faith and religious practice an important source of support in adjusting to her husband's death.[26] Joan often comments on the importance of her faith in dealing with grief. In the following interview excerpt, she reflects on the role of faith in helping her come to terms with her mother's death when Joan was eighteen:

> Well, as I think about my life, all my life has been based on Christian belief…In my late teens my mother died. And I had a serious boyfriend at that time; just before my mother died, he and I broke up. So I was feeling pretty down one day, and I guess just kind of heartbroken. So I knelt beside my bed, I was at home by myself. And I prayed about this and just asked the Lord to help me through all this. And suddenly there was such a warmth over my body (smiles and raises her hands to her shoulders and moves them down to her knees) I'll *never* forget it. And I felt complete release. I got up and went into the other room and sat down to the old

organ–and I sang the song "Take My Life and Let It Be," and the tears just rolled...Of course you know during our lives we have a lot of wonderful experiences as well as sad and so forth. But that [faith, religious experience], to me, is where I have gained my strength and [why I] have been a happy person all my life.

For many older adults, religious beliefs and practices are highly effective in coping with negative life events such as illness, one's own death, and the death of a spouse. Joan's faith, expressed through her participation in her congregation and daily devotional time, has provided a sense of stability in the face of the tremendous changes accompanying widowhood. A number of researchers have found the kind of positive correlation between religious belief and coping behavior in late life that Joan describes here.[27] Among the practices that promote a sense of well-being among older adults are church attendance, Bible study, and prayer, all of which also correlate positively with an increased sense of well-being for older adults.[28]

In addition to her religious faith and involvement in her church community, involvement with friends, family, and volunteer activities provides additional social support and a sense of purpose. Even in the midst of her grief, Joan reports many enjoyable experiences in her life, including her relationship with her grandchildren.

We have five grandchildren and two great-grandchildren, and one of our granddaughters is pregnant for the first time. And they are just the smartest, sweetest, best little children you ever know [laughs]. You know, they are. It is interesting how you love your grandchildren and then the great grandchildren...Well, of course, the grandchildren are so wonderful, because all you can do is love them and they visit you and then you can send them home and all that sort of thing, but they are very dear. Grandchildren are just so special.

Joan also has enjoyed music all her life and has often sung in the church choir or played the piano for church services. She still returns to her former church to sing in the choir at Christmas time and other special events and plays the piano on occasion for the vesper services at her new home. Music is just one of the ways she volunteers at the retirement community where she now resides.

Well, I will continue to be very busy here. I have just accepted a chairmanship of a committee here. And as long as I can, I will be going back to my church. Whether I'll still be driving then, of course I don't know. But I will just continue to be a part of this organization and do what I can. And there's some people here in their nineties and so forth—I told you—and they're as sharp as they can be. And I just pray that if I live, I will continue to be able to think and remember...

You know, there are so many things on the program here. And, of course, we exercise three days a week, besides a walk. I was trying to walk with somebody today. And I play the piano once a month for Vespers.

Joan's volunteer activities and her family relationships form part of a well-developed support system, which research consistently shows to be an important factor in a positive adjustment to widowhood.[29]

Joan seems to be making a good adjustment to widowhood. She was assisted in this adjustment by the pastoral care she received from both her local church pastor and the chaplain of the senior housing facility where she now resides. Joan has been able to make good use of her external and internal resources in moving through her grief and adjusting to this major life change, which includes a changing sense of identity from wife to widow.

Joan's experience embodies the good news that for a majority of women the experience of widowhood does not conform to the social myths about widowhood as "very restricted, isolated, or dependent lifestyles in a limited social life space."[30] Yet widowhood is unique for each woman and does involve real losses and significant changes in one's life. Although each woman will adjust to widowhood in her own way according to the internal and external resources available to her, the church community can assist in this adjustment by helping women to identify their internal resources and offering external support through the process of grief and identity restructuring that accompanies widowhood.

Joan's story also reminds us that for many older women widowhood may be preceded by a period of caregiving, which has its own challenges and stresses. As the population ages, the number of older adults needing care will increase. Church communities can become part of a support network for caregivers in their congregations and help link caregivers to other services in the larger community. We will return to this issue in more detail in chapter 7.

Relational Practices of Care with Widowed Women

Just as with ever-single women, relational practices of care with widowed women begin with assessing their relational networks. For widows, these networks may include adult children, grandchildren, and perhaps great-grandchildren. Knowing something about the tenor of these relationships and the geographic and emotional availability of these extended family members helps us evaluate the family support systems at hand. As we saw in Joan's case, once through the initial period of loss and grief, most women make the adjustment to widowhood quite well. Following this transition, relational practices of care are similar to those with ever-single women: providing support for the significant relationships in a woman's life and assisting in expanding communities of support when these have been reduced through loss or death.

Providing care at the death of someone's husband or life partner is one of the primary tasks of relational practices of care with widowed women.[31] In most cases this care will be provided by a pastor or designated pastoral caregiver with some knowledge of grief and loss and with skills in short-term crisis intervention. In situations in which a death is anticipated, a pastoral caregiver may have the opportunity to provide care and support during the period of anticipatory grief prior to the death. In many cases, pastoral care begins with the death and the planning of the funeral or memorial service.

Relational Practices of Care at the Death of a Spouse or Life Partner

Ritualizing a loss is often an important part of healing. In the case of widowhood, the ritual of the funeral is generally expected.[32] Clergy are often the first helping professionals to attend to new widows through their roles in conducting funeral services. Clergy and other pastoral caregivers need to be educated about the processes of normal grief and complicated grief. With this knowledge, they are in a prime position to provide opportunities for early intervention and appropriate referral in cases of complicated grief. The impact of the funeral service itself should not be underestimated. Funerals often mark the official initiation into public dimensions of the grieving process and the role of widow. Identifying the religious rituals that are most meaningful to a woman and her family and designing a funeral service that responds to their unique religious and emotional needs can facilitate movement through the grief process. Thoughtful pastoral care in the acute stages of grief can make a significant difference in the longer-term resolution of grief.

Two forms of care are important at the time of death: the more traditional pastoral care model of one-to-one counseling around issues of grief and loss, and congregational support, expressed more informally and often provided through practical and emotional support. As noted earlier, more formal pastoral care often begins with the funeral. Short-term pastoral counseling may be appropriate in the first few weeks of grief. It may be important for a woman to tell the story of how the death occurred as she seeks to make sense of the event. A range of emotions may accompany the loss, including relief and sometimes guilt, especially when the death has been preceded by a long illness or brings an end to an abusive marriage. Caregivers must remain open to whatever feelings emerge and assist the woman in moving through these.[33] Helping women understand the grieving process, including the physical toll it can take, is an important dimension of care.

Because of the way grief unfolds, follow-up care at three months, six months, and the anniversary of the death can facilitate positive movement through grief. It takes about three months for the reality of the death to take hold, and at six months issues of loneliness and isolation often arise. At the anniversary of the death, mourners can experience intense emotions, which is a fairly common response to the anniversary but often leaves a woman feeling as if she has not made progress and is back in acute grief. Unless there are factors that complicate the grief or have interrupted the grief process, this is rarely the case.[34]

Creating Communities of Support

The support of others who have experienced partner loss can be a positive factor in adjustment to bereavement.[35] Many churches now offer short-term grief groups for the recently bereaved. Such groups are valuable not only because they offer a structured environment for constructive grief work but also because they often become the basis of an informal ongoing support network. Widowhood involves a change in role from married to single; however, the role of widow is not well defined in contemporary U.S. culture. Some women find that they no longer fit in comfortably with married couples, yet their experience of being single is different from that of ever-single or divorced women. A widow should be encouraged to maintain relationships in existence prior to her husband's death and also to expand her network of support. This can be accomplished by linking up with others who have similar interests in the church. Involvement in educational programs and outreach projects often provides an opportunity to make such connections. The church might also provide opportunities for women to connect with other widows who are experiencing a similar transition.

Congregations can play a critical role at such life passages and can be important communities of support for widowed women. Lay members of congregations are often adept at providing practical support, such as the provision of meals or help with household tasks. Practical help received early in the grief process can make a positive difference in the adjustment to widowhood. Both "affective," or emotional, and "instrumental," or practical, help received early in the grief process have a significant impact on later mental health and adjustment to bereavement.[36] Many churches provide informal networks for such emotional and practical support. One of the most common forms of practical help is the provision of a meal for surviving family members after a funeral. This reminds the new widow that she is a part of a larger community of faith, which can be an ongoing source of social support and material sustenance to her. This sharing around the family table following a funeral can be reminiscent of communion, a central ritual and liturgical act that reminds us how we are interconnected with one another as part of the Christian community.

Often the practical help provided by congregations at a partner's death is informal; it comes out of a Sunday school class or another group within the church in which a woman has been active. The formation of more formal networks to provide both emotional and practical help early in the grieving process can be particularly important for women in the church who are not a part of these informal networks of support. Women who have been the primary caretakers for ill spouses have often dropped out of these networks and can be easily overlooked.

The practical help offered by a congregation following a partner's death can be expanded beyond the traditional provision of the funeral meal. One of the adjustments that a woman must make at widowhood is assuming responsibility for the tasks that the partner previously performed. Although most women usually figure out how to handle these additional tasks, some of which may be unfamiliar to them, at first they can be quite overwhelming. Congregations might provide various kinds of practical help to newly widowed women, such as assistance in financial matters, home maintenance and repair, shopping, and other aspects of daily living. This help may not need to be long term but can be offered in the first six to eight weeks following the death during the most acute grief. Some lay members may feel inadequate at providing emotional support at the time of death yet are quite willing and able to offer practical assistance. It is important that such instrumental help not be devalued by an overemphasis on the counseling model of care.

In addition to offering women assistance in taking on the responsibilities once performed by the husband or partner, the church can also encourage women to gain new skills needed to complete these tasks. Linking women with resources in the community is an important dimension to the practice of creating and sustaining communities of support. Programs such as the Shepherd's Center, senior centers, or community colleges often offer short-term courses in home maintenance or financial management.[37] As a woman masters new tasks, she typically increases her sense of competence and confidence, which may lead to the construction of a positive narrative of widowhood.

Linking Narrative and Relational Practices

The transition to widowhood, which marks a major change in a woman's relational network, also requires a revision of the subjective and intersubjective dimension of her self-narrative. The church can facilitate or enhance this narrative reconstruction both through the one-on-one care provided immediately following the loss and through its educational and formational ministries. Women who have a sense of identity in addition to the traditional roles of wife and mother seemed to fare better in this task of narrative revision. Through its educational and outreach ministries, as well as opportunities for leadership, the church might help older women find interests and identities outside these traditional roles while not diminishing their importance. Congregational leaders can actively encourage widowed women to become involved in a variety of ministries within the church community. It is important that these opportunities for ministry expand beyond the traditional roles of volunteer secretarial help. Involvement in various outreach ministries, such as assisting in the homeless shelter, or involvement in other hands-on projects, such as construction of a Habitat for Humanity home, may provide opportunities for women to both expand their relational networks and develop new skills and new competencies that contribute to a new self-narrative.

So in addition to providing assistance in the immediate aftermath of death, the church can also provide a variety of opportunities for a woman's continued engagement in life and the faith community. For this to occur, the church must challenge sexist and ageist attitudes and stereotypes about women. This includes questioning developmental schemas that might shape our expectations about what kind of growth and development are possible for older women.

Widows are not the only women who experience relationship losses resulting in revised life narratives and changes in relational networks. Divorce also results in the loss of a life partner and requires narrative revision. We now turn to the story of Katherine, an older woman coping with the aftermath of a mid-life divorce.

Older Women and Divorce

Katherine is proud of her independence and of building a life for herself after a difficult divorce in her fifties that followed many years of marital conflict. Now divorced eighteen years, "divorced woman" is not her primary self-identification, but she is aware that this status does impact her experience of aging.

Katherine: A Life of Her Own

Katherine is a sixty-nine-year-old African American woman. She is slim, elegantly dressed in a sage-green silk blouse and dark gray slacks. Katherine is very active, energetic, and intelligent, and her education and experiences reflect her sense of compassion for others. Upon retiring from a career in teaching, Katherine relocated to the southeast to be near her children and grandchildren. She has now been single for eighteen years following thirty-two years of marriage.

Katherine was born in 1933 in the rural southeastern United States and was one of eight children. After her mother's death when she was seven, Katherine was raised by her aunt as an only child. She attended public schools and eventually entered one of the historically black colleges at the age of fifteen. At sixteen, Katherine fell in love, and she married her husband a couple of years later; they moved often because of her husband's job. Katherine and her husband eventually settled in the southeast, where she raised four children– one daughter and three sons. Katherine and her husband shared a commitment to the pursuit of higher education, and he earned a doctoral degree in 1961, though not without facing significant resistance and prejudice in the process. Following thirty-two years of marriage and a year of legal separation, Katherine divorced her husband. The marriage had become increasingly difficult as his long-standing psychological problems, complicated by the ongoing strain of racism, worsened. His refusal to seek treatment and her concern for her then ten-year-old son finally led her to make the difficult decision to divorce her husband.

Following her divorce she moved to the Midwest and completed a master's degree in special education; she taught for several years there. Katherine now resides in a town house near her children and seven grandchildren. Unfortunately, the school district where she taught for a number of years had severe financial difficulties; as a result, her retirement income is very limited. Her restricted income presents challenges, yet she is very independent and reluctant to let her children know the reality of her financial situation. She places great importance on her faith and prayers to see her through difficult times. She also stresses that older people need to be reminded that they can still contribute to society and that the greatest gift a minister can give to aging persons is to listen to them and value them for "their gifts and talents and challenges and needs."

DISCUSSION. Katherine is among the 8 percent of women over the age of sixty-five who are divorced. These percentages are likely to increase as the baby boom generation ages; some researchers predict that nearly one fifth of this baby boom cohort will be divorced.[38] As an African American woman, Katherine is in a group that has a divorce rate slightly higher than the population as a whole.[39] Katherine was divorced at age fifty-one after thirty-two years of marriage; thus her experience was quite typical. The majority of mid-life and older women who divorce do so between the ages of forty and sixty; only 2 percent of divorces involve women over the age of sixty.[40]

Katherine has made a good adjustment to divorce over time in terms of life satisfaction, as do many older women. A 1993 study of more than three hundred recently divorced women age forty to seventy-five confirmed that the majority of these women regain positive feelings about themselves, make new friends, and discover a new freedom to define their sense of self following divorce.[41] When divorce follows a long and turbulent marriage, as in Katherine's case, it is more likely to provide a sense of greater safety and freedom. It is common for a period of grief and recovery to precede a positive long-term adjustment to divorce.

Divorce, always a difficult process, is often complicated for older women by the length of the marriage and by social attitudes toward divorce. Katherine was raised during a time when divorce was more stigmatized than it is today. So it is not at all unusual for older women to initiate the divorce process only after many years of marital unhappiness, incompatibility, cruelty, infidelity, or other significant problems.[42] Older women who do not initiate the divorce are often surprised by it even though they may report turbulent marriages involving infidelity and alcoholism.[43]

Divorce, like widowhood, marks the end of a marriage, and even though the circumstance may be quite different, grief attends divorce just as it does widowhood. Divorce grief can have a somewhat different character from that of grief following the death of a spouse and may be complicated by feelings of abandonment, betrayal, or fear. Some women may feel great relief following divorce, mingled with real sadness for broken dreams and the end of family life. Divorce may bring not only the loss of the spouse but also loss of access to in-laws and other extended family members with whom one may have had positive relationships. The stigma of divorce and the grief of other family members may add to the emotional turmoil of a woman who is divorcing.

In Katherine's case, she was affected by the reaction of other family members to her divorce to such an extent that she relocated to another city following her divorce. She often felt as if she had to care for others, as well as herself and her children. She reflects on her decision to move because of the added emotional burden of the reaction of family members.

> I moved...since every time I came this way people were grieving over the events of our lives. I found myself trying to console them when I needed to have a fresh opportunity to heal. So that's why I moved. I had aunts and cousins who were more supportive there [in the new place] than my relatives at home were able to be.

Restricted finances and limited opportunities for improving one's economic position are challenges that face many older divorced women. Divorce has more negative economic consequences on older women than does widowhood. These older women are less likely to live independently and own their own homes. The financial setbacks accompanying divorce put older women at a disadvantage compared with divorced men and other marital groups. Although most ever-single women have worked most of their lives, and widowed women can often rely on their husbands' retirement income, older divorced women may have entered the work force late and have limited retirement benefits.

Katherine is in a better position than some women because she owns her own home and has some retirement income. However, she finds that the financial difficulties she faces as a divorced women present a significant challenge:

> The biggest challenges are being a single aging person, not allowing myself to feel overwhelmed with things that I can easily do [for myself, when I try].
>
> Well, housekeeping things, you know. Coming back here I bought a townhouse because I retired, took early retirement, actually, because the school district went broke. My income

is very limited. And whenever I allow myself to focus on what I don't have, which I can easily do, I become very anxious. And I'm so proud. I don't want my children to know. And I get fussed at and I get in trouble and they do have to know. But, you know, I can spin my wheels unnecessarily. And I think this is an issue with many older people.

PASTORAL ASSESSMENT. Having been independent much of her life, Katherine now finds it difficult to rely financially on her children. Independence emerged as an important theme for Katherine, as well as many of the women interviewed. This fierce sense of independence certainly reflects American cultural values, but it can also be problematic in late life. Parents who have generously cared for children often find it difficult to allow children to care for them, financially, emotionally, or physically when the need arises. Katherine's reluctance to accept financial assistance from her children has been a source of conflict with her children on several occasions.

In addition to financial challenges, older divorced women are faced with the challenge of redefining themselves and finding a sense of identity outside of the marriage. Katherine has found that her faith and her involvement in a local congregation provide support as well as sense of meaning and purpose for her as a single woman. As an expression of her new identity, Katherine chose to join a church that was quite different from the black Baptist church of her childhood and also different from the churches she attended during her marriage.

When I moved back here, I tried my best to reconnect with some of the churches I'd grown up in because I was Baptist. I only came to United Methodism upon marriage. And I think it's a true adage: you cannot go home [again]. I was living near this church and started visiting. And there was such an outpouring of welcome and interest, I felt a genuine caring that said, "Won't you join us?" And because I suppose my needs have gone through a metamorphosis in terms of what I feel. I need at this stage of my life to grow spiritually. I say it this way: I no longer think that God needs a lot of noise. I like a still, small voice. I do a lot of meditation and introspection.

So the worship here—and that was the first thing I was aware of—gave me a period that I could listen to myself, my needs, as well as God speaking.

A part of Katherine's new identity is a call to bridging racial difference. She now attends a congregation that is largely European American, though committed to inclusion. She feels that only by truly knowing each other can differences and prejudices be overcome. Her experiences of prejudice, which included growing up under Jim Crow laws in the South and often being the only African American teacher (and person) in schools in the Midwest, have convinced her that bridging differences is a part of her vocation at this point in her life.

The church has continued to be a place of support for Katherine, even though her religious practice and spiritual needs have changed somewhat over the years. Katherine reminds us that we should not assume that spiritual growth or religious needs remain the same over the life course, nor that all older women have the same spiritual needs. Attention to these spiritual needs is an important part of pastoral care, as Katherine suggests:

> Most older people have reached a level of appreciation of their spirituality, and a pastor is a representative of an agent who can deal with this aspect of their lives. They [pastors] have unique opportunities because they are non-threatening...And I see this [listening] as their [pastors'] biggest challenge and their greatest charge.

Relational Practices of Care with Divorced Women

Many of the forms of care relevant for ever-single and widowed women, such as attending to the relational networks and noting the extent of women's communities of support, are appropriate for older divorced woman as well. Divorced and widowed woman share the experience of the loss of a life partner. At the point of the loss of the relationship, both can benefit from assistance in recognizing and moving through the grief process. As a general rule, however, congregations seem to be more responsive to issues of grief following the death of a spouse than at divorce.

An often overlooked aspect of care at the time of divorce is the need of some women to ritualize this loss, just as a funeral ritualizes a loss. Many older women who divorce come from a generation in which divorce was stigmatized. Because marriages often end after many years of difficulty and on occasion abuse, the church can assist in the process of healing through helping women design rituals that acknowledge the breaking of the covenant while releasing them from the obligations of promises they are no longer able to keep. Such a ritual might help older women overcome a sense of shame and failure that often accompanies divorce.

Another form of ministry that congregations offer following the death of a spouse that we don't think to offer at the time of a divorce is practical assistance in adjusting to the loss of a spouse. Just as widowed women take on the former responsibilities of husbands, so too do divorced women. The various forms of practical assistance discussed as a form of care for widowed women are also relevant for divorced women. Because women often face greater financial hardship following divorce than do men, practical assistance, such as helping a divorced woman set up a new household, can be a powerful expression of care.

Just as widowed women can benefit from grief support groups, divorce recovery groups can be a source of support for women experiencing this transition. I have discovered that one of the most powerful dimensions of this ministry is helping women understand the stages of grief that follow divorce, even in cases where divorce provided welcome relief from an intolerable situation. Such groups, offered as part of a congregation's ministry of care, can be led by a pastor or trained lay members and signal to divorced women that there is a place for them in this community. Divorced women may experience some churches as primarily family-oriented and have a difficult time feeling comfortable in such a congregation following the disruption of family life that divorce represents.

Unlike widowed women, divorced women often have some kind of ongoing relationships with former spouses, especially when there are children and grandchildren. In most cases the conflicts leading to the end of a marriage are not resolved following divorce. As a result, the need for ongoing contact with a former spouse at holiday time or for children's birthdays can be quite stressful. This situation can be further complicated if both spouses participate in the same congregation. Simply being aware of this situation or offering informal pastoral support around stressful family events can be expressions of care.

Like widowed women, divorced women face a narrative reconstruction of a life story, particularly the future dimensions, following a divorce. A woman's sense of self-esteem is often compromised by a divorce, especially following a long marriage. Once again we see how narrative practices of care intertwine with relational practices. Not only do divorced women need to come to a new understanding of self, but also the expansion of relational networks and communities of support is essential in this process. Because many women experience divorce as a failure of relationship regardless of the circumstances, helping a woman to recognize how she has maintained other important relationships in her life can be an important part of narrative reconstruction. This revision of narrative may occur in informal pastoral conversation or in the context of a divorce recovery group, as well as in the context of more formal short-term pastoral counseling that may follow divorce.

As Katherine reminds us, older single women's lives are individual and unique. Although it is important to attend to the particular needs of women related to their status as ever-single, widowed, or divorced, older women's lives are defined by more than their relational status. Through relational practices, caregivers acknowledge the importance of—and tend to the matrix of—interpersonal, family, and communal relationships in which older women live their lives. In the next chapter we turn to tending relationships and creating communities of support with married and partnered women.

CHAPTER 6

Tending Relationships
Marriage, Partnership, Family, and Friends

A palpable buzz filed the air as soon as I walked through the doors of Kingston Place that day. "Have you heard? There's going to be a wedding!" Joan, one of the other residents of Kingston Place, an independent living facility for older adults, filled me in on the news. Two of the residents, Mary, age eighty-four, and Jackson, ninety-two, were getting married in the dining hall later that week. Everyone was excited!

Shaped as we are by cultural assumptions of aging, those of us who are younger may consider a marriage in late life as a curiosity. This reaction is not uncommon. In fact, one of the local news stations heard of the upcoming nuptials and came to interview Mary and Jackson for a human-interest story. Why does such a marriage catch us off-guard? Marriages of older adults are less common than those of younger people, but I think this is not the only reason for our surprise. True, we probably wonder why two people would want to commit to the future, when in our estimation, there seems to be little of it left. But the primary reason for our surprise is typically the assumption that older adults are no longer interested in the companionship, intimacy, and sexuality that a partner provides. Although there is more to a marriage than a sexual relationship, this form of physical intimacy is an important element.

Although many older women will find themselves without a life partner at some point, marriage or partnership continues to provide the primary relational context for many other women. I am using the combined terms *marriage* and *partnership* to remind us that marriage is only one form that intimate, committed relationships may take. Hearing stories of marriage and partnership provides an opportunity to explore intimacy and sexuality in this context, although both these remain important to women regardless of relational status.

We begin this chapter with three portraits of intimate relationships in late life. We return first to the story of Mary and Jackson, who help us discover the joys of a new marriage in later life. As Ann and Elizabeth share their story, we are reminded that marriage is not the only form of partnership for women; in their case we hear about their shared lives as two older lesbian women in a long-term committed relationship. The third portrait is of Rose, who reminds us that growth is a lifelong process and who shares her experience of renewal in a long-term marriage. The three portraits are followed by a pastoral assessment of issues presented in these three cases and a discussion of relevant relational practices of care. Finally, to close the two chapters on older women's relationships and related practices of care, we explore the roles of motherhood and women's friendships, vital dimensions of the lives of older women both single and partnered.

Remarriage in Later Life

We often perceive remarriage for older women as an exceptional event. Such a response is due in part to the demographic realities; older women significantly outnumber older men and have less chance of remarrying. As noted, unarticulated assumptions about aging and sexuality also affect our views of marriage in late life: We question why people age eighty and ninety would desire to marry; surely it can't be sexual desire. The popular image of late-life marriage or partnership is of a primarily companionate relationship, with twin beds or separate bedrooms.

For older adults who do remarry, the desire for intimacy, in many forms, is the primary motivation. Intimacy includes emotional closeness, as well as physical and sexual intimacy, all of which continue to be important to many older adults. Because of our ageist attitudes, we often do not expect older adults to remain interested in sexual intimacy. As a result, some adult children may have a hard time thinking of an older parent as a sexual being and may resist or try to block a remarriage.

The support of extended family, although always an important factor in the decision to marry, may be especially crucial in an older couple's consideration of remarriage. The story of Mary and Jackson provides a portrait of one couple's courtship and marriage, both heartily supported by family, friends, the faith community, and the residential community in which they live.

Mary and Jackson

Mary is eighty-four and Jackson is ninety-two; both are of European American descent. They had been married about four months at the time of the interview. Mary had responded to my flyer posted at her retirement home that sought participants for my interview study with women over the age of sixty-five. Mary had been married previously but had been widowed for nearly thirty years. After deciding that living on her own was becoming increasingly difficult, she relocated to the retirement home where she now lives to be in a more supportive environment and nearer to her children. She became quite active in the community after relocating and soon met Jackson through her involvement in the choir and other activities. Having faced and survived serious illness earlier in her life, she is grateful for each day and continues to find life full of surprises, including her recent marriage.

DISCUSSION. Mary and Jackson, both widowed, met in the choir at the senior residence where they now both live, shortly after Mary moved into Kingston Place. Jackson and his former wife had been married for more than sixty years, and he had been widowed less than a year. Mary, however, had been widowed for thirty years. Mary and Jackson reflect some typical patterns in remarriage. Men are likely to remarry much sooner than women and generally marry younger women.

As they stood side by side in the choir, they discovered a mutual love for music and a shared faith. Jackson, who has some visual impairment, depended on Mary to hand him the hymnal and described to me how he would let his hand linger just a little longer each time she handed him the book. They married about four months after they met, about which he remarked, "You don't have much time to waste at our age." Both reported that they faced no objections from their families; indeed, their announcement was met with much celebration. Mary's granddaughter, who was studying for the ordained ministry, participated in the marriage ceremony.

Mary comments that this late-life marriage came as quite a pleasant surprise to her. After being widowed for thirty years, she is enjoying the emotional closeness, intimacy, and companionship. Jackson, like many older men who remarry, had been single a much shorter period, about a year. Men are more likely to take the initiative in the new relationship because they generally have a harder time adjusting to the loss of a spouse than women do.[1] Jackson had been his wife's primary caretaker for a number of years during her illness and until her death, and was in that sense already grieving and therefore somewhat prepared to move on into a new relationship. After this lengthy period of caretaking, he notes the greater degree of reciprocity in his relationship with Mary and also reports his enjoyment of their shared interests. Mary reflects on her new marriage and the sense of connection with each other that they both enjoy.

> Now I'm married, and very happily so, a most unusual–unexpected, I guess, not unusual–event. Maybe unusual, too. I think that [our shared faith] was part–a big part–of our courtship because Jackson loved to talk about his churches and the things that happened, and I loved to listen. And I got to know him a lot more just by listening.
>
> So sometimes I think my marriage is a dream. It's not for real. But it wasn't a dream I ever thought of having, I tell you. But it's been a wonderful experience. And if it continues and we even have one more date, it was all worth it. It was all quite a wonderful experience. A wonderful change.

Not only was the marriage of Mary and Jackson news in their immediate residential community, it was news in the larger community. The reporter from one of the local television stations who interviewed them for a human-interest story asked Mary, "What do appreciate most about your marriage?" She replied, "Well, we laugh at the things we can do and we laugh at the things we cannot do." Although this comment was oblique, it was clear from further conversation that Mary was making reference to issues of intimacy and sexuality. The idea of two people of advanced old age marrying was apparently a newsworthy event. However, the suggestion that this couple was also enjoying the physical and sexual aspects of the marriage was not considered appropriate for prime-time news. Mary herself noted that these comments were not included in the broadcast of the interview. Such ambivalent attitudes toward late-life marriage and intimacy are not uncommon and reflect our stereotypical assumptions about old age.

PASTORAL ASSESSMENT. Mary and Jackson remind us that the needs for companionship, intimacy, and sexuality are not confined to any one period of life. Their example challenges us to see older single and partnered adults as fully human and, contrary to popular assumptions, often still quite interested in intimacy and sexuality.[2] All too often, we assume that older adults have lost either sexual interest or ability; those who do express such interest we often label dirty old women or men. The assumptions about sexuality and late life reveal a bias that our experiences, desires, and needs in later life are somehow discontinuous with our experiences in or earlier life. Our desire to retain a continuous and coherent sense of self over time, as suggested by continuity theory, contradicts such assumptions.

Unfortunately, the decision of an older couple to remarry may be met with resistance by adult children and may generate discord in some families, not least because of such assumptions. Mary and Jackson are fortunate to have the support of their immediate communities and their families; family support, a good adjustment to age-related changes, and sufficient income all contribute to the success of remarriage in late life.

Relational Practices

Because family support or lack of it may have significant influence on an older couple's decision to marry, pastors can tend the relationships of older adults through mediating family resistance to marriage in later life. Beyond attitudes to sexuality, family resistance to a remarriage may have to do with concern over financial matters such as inheritance. Resistance may also be a result of an adult child being unwilling to allow a parent to change or expecting her to be available exclusively to the adult child. This may more likely be the case with women who have been single for some time prior to the remarriage. The first step in addressing the resistance is to assess the nature of the resistance.

In situations where financial issues are the primary concern, pastoral care providers can encourage a woman to draw up a prenuptial agreement and current will that address issues of inheritance and support for children from the previous marriage. These documents should then be discussed with adult children, if necessary with the help of the pastor. Sometimes financial issues are the presenting concern in resistance to a remarriage, but the underlying issue is fear of losing access to a parent or concern over a parent's judgment.

The task of care at this point is to uncover the unspoken future narratives that adult children have about their parent's life. Ageist assumptions that might be shaping these narratives and restricting the choices of a parent need to be uncovered as a part of the narrative reconstruction in this situation. If a remarriage involves a move or relocation, adult children might fear loss of access to the parent; to address this, pastoral caregivers can encourage adult children to raise these concerns with parents, so that together they can fashion an alternative future narrative. Attending to these narratives allows us to tend to the family relationships that can provide significant support for the new marital relationship.

Affirming sexuality and intimacy as legitimate needs of older women pertains to all older women, single or partnered. What blocks our affirmation of intimacy and sexuality in late life are our narrow definitions of these terms. We tend to reduce intimacy to physical intimacy and sexuality to genital sexual activity. Contributing to a limited view of sexuality are strands within the Christian traditions that have associated sexuality with sin and restricted the genital expression of sexual desire to the purpose of procreation. These religious attitudes may stand behind our objection to sexually active older women.

Sexuality is a fundamental dimension of our embodied human existence; our very femaleness or maleness is an expression of sexuality quite apart from whether we are sexually active. Sensuality, desire, a longing for an intense connection, or a temporary merging of self and other are all expressions of sexuality. As ethicist James Nelson affirms, sexuality involves "our minds, our feelings, our wills, our memories, indeed our self-understandings and powers as embodied persons."[3] Sexuality is one expression of our relational natures and of our capacity to love. Older women who are sexually inactive through choice or circumstance are still sexual beings.

Reduced physical intimacy and activity in old age may be a result of limited opportunity or physical ailment, but social attitudes toward sexual activity in late life also have a powerful limiting affect. Redefining sexuality and sexual pleasure to highlight affection, touch, companionship, and various forms of physical pleasure can be liberating for older adults. Mary and Jackson, for example, laugh over the things they can do and those they can no longer do, suggesting that whether or not intercourse is a still a possibility, physical and sexual intimacy is still important to them. Broadening our understanding of sexuality and affirming it as fundamental to human existence allow us to laugh and celebrate with Mary and Jackson.

Committed Partnerships

Marriage is only one form of intimate relationship that older adults may choose. Some older women may have an intimate and sexual relationship with a male partner but choose not to marry or cohabit because of complicating financial issues such as pension and Social Security benefits and concerns about inheritance or because of resistance and lack of support from adult children. Some older women are in long-term committed lesbian relationships. These relationships are often invisible to us because of assumptions about older women's sexuality. Somehow, we find it difficult to imagine that the sweet-looking white-haired lady sitting next to us on the bus could be a lesbian. Ann and Elizabeth help broaden our images of older women and their intimate relationships.

Older lesbian women have received little attention by researchers, including feminists. The literature that does exist is primarily in the form of personal reflections.[4] Ann and Elizabeth, whose story we first encountered in chapter 4, add their voices to these few reflections as they share their experience of being committed partners in later life.

Ann and Elizabeth: Women Together

Ann, seventy, and her partner of eleven years, Elizabeth, sixty-five, live in a rural community not far from a large city. Both families have been fairly accepting of Ann and Elizabeth's relationship. Ann's two daughters accept her relationship with Elizabeth and are able to talk openly about it. Elizabeth's family, a son and daughter and four grandchildren, has given more limited support. Her daughter is fairly supportive, but her son and daughter-in-law do not allow her to talk to the grandchildren about her relationship with Ann. They have also found support for their relationship in their Unitarian congregation with a group of women with whom they meet for a monthly "potluck."

DISCUSSION. Ann and Elizabeth represent a small but growing and often overlooked group of women: older lesbians. These two women grew up in an era when homosexuality carried greater taboos and was less readily accepted than it is today. Like many older lesbian women, they followed the expected social patterns for women, marrying and having children. The movements for women's liberation and gay rights provided an environment in which they could claim an acceptance of their sexual identities. Many older lesbian women have come to an awareness of their sexual identity only in mid-life. This awareness may come after the launching of children into adulthood; it may come after the end of a marriage or precipitate the end of a marriage. Like many older lesbian couples, Ann and Elizabeth have been together for a number of years.

Although Ann and Elizabeth are mostly invisible to the larger culture, they are fortunate to have relatively positive relationships with their families and are a part of a liberal and supportive church community. These factors of community and family support are as important for the success of same-sex relationships as for heterosexual relationships.

Ann and Elizabeth reflect on their lives together.

Ann: We're family. Elizabeth's family is mine and my family is hers. We're very blended now after ten years–

Elizabeth: Ten-and-three-quarter years.

Ann: But we also share the tasks and share the upkeep, I think, pretty equitably. I do probably more of the outdoor work. I maintain the vegetable garden and do the composting and that sort of thing. Elizabeth does more of the cooking. She does most of the cooking and I do the cleanup. So we share household tasks.

Elizabeth: Well, I feel one of my great blessings is that I'm in, I think, very good health for my age. I have some arthritis. I don't take any medications at all. I take herbal supplements and vitamins. I believe like Dean says in that book *Love and Survival,* if you have a network of people that care about you and if you think positive thoughts and you eat well and exercise enough, you'll live a happy, old, long life.

Ann: That's more important than the genes, they're finding out now. The genetic stuff is important, yes, but we can change that a whole lot with the way that we live. And that's one of my goals now: to keep living a good life and be grateful for what I have. And I am. I am very grateful. I have a partner whom I love and who cares for me and cooks gourmet meals.

Pastoral Assessment. As Ann and Elizabeth talk about their lives, we discover that they have the same concerns as the rest of us, regardless of our sexual identity, such as sharing household tasks and maintaining their health. We are also reminded that in addition to a supportive partner, self-care and a network of friends have a positive effect on well-being in later life–as they do throughout the life cycle. Such awareness reminds us to be attentive to all aspects of lesbian women's lives, and not limit our care only to issues of sexuality.

Ann and Elizabeth enjoy a relatively high degree of support for their partnership. They are fortunate to have the acceptance, if not the full backing, of their families, and they have found a church community and network of friends that supports them in their lives together. This support may have something to do with the stability of their relationship over time. Other older lesbian women in committed relationships may not be so fortunate.

Relational Practices of Care

Relational practices of care with lesbian couples begin with the recognition that contrary to popular belief, most older lesbians are coupled.[5] Congregational affirmation of the partner status of the couple is particularly crucial when women are isolated from their families. The church community that welcomes older lesbian couples to full participation in the life of the congregation and provides a community of support can become a "safety net" when a couple experiences periods of stress. An important role of the pastor, as well as other key leaders, is assisting the congregation in a journey toward full celebration of such nontraditional relationships. Because the institutional church has been reluctant to acknowledge the legitimacy of same-sex partnerships, significant theological and pastoral work may need to be done with a largely heterosexual congregation in order to create a specifically welcoming and affirming environment for lesbian couples.[6] Pastors will also need to examine their own attitudes and views as part of this process.[7]

Lack of social support can affect the stability of lesbian partnerships. Partnerships lasting forty years or more, as some marriages do, are rare. Heterosexual couples, however, experience social expectations to stay married. Lesbian couples experience neither the social pressure nor the support to maintain such long-term partnerships. So although some partnerships last a relatively long period, it is not uncommon for lesbian women to move through a series of committed partnerships lasting from a few years to decades.[8] Awareness of this reality can alert us to the need for pastoral care when relationships come to an end.

Women in same-sex partnerships who lose partners through death or through the ending of the relationships are less visible and therefore arguably more in need than divorced or widowed women. Because these women have many of the same needs as widowed or divorced women, many of the strategies suggested in the previous chapter for providing support and care for the divorced or widowed are also appropriate for lesbian women experiencing partner loss. However, lesbian women experiencing partner loss generally have less social support than heterosexual women at the time of loss. The emotional impact of partner loss may be magnified if the loss goes unrecognized, or if the relationship is not recognized as legitimate. Such unacknowledged loss often complicates the grieving process.[9] In addition to the loss of one's partner and companion, lesbian women may also experience financial losses at death or the dissolution of a relationship if the partners' finances were intertwined.

Unlike Mary and Jackson, Ann and Elizabeth cannot assume that they will automatically inherit from each other or that they will have any say about health care issues at the end of life. Ann and Elizabeth have taken steps to provide for their children and each other at the time of death, but laws governing inheritance and end of life care vary from state to state. Church communities can be advocates for older women by advocating for state laws that allow older women to make legal provisions for a partner at the end of life. One such legal provision might include laws governing beneficiaries of employment benefits, including retirement benefits.

Ann and Elizabeth, who have been together for eleven years, have no doubt weathered the ups and downs of any intimate relationship and have made the transition to retirement together. Lesbian partnerships, like marriage, change over time, and retirement can be a catalyst for change in a relationship, as we saw in the previous chapter. Retirement can present new challenges to a couple; it can also be a time of new freedom and growth. Ann and Elizabeth were concerned about the impact retirement would have on their relationship, as well as their quality of life. Like Rose and Jim, they found that having more time together, as well as more time to pursue individual interests, strengthened their relationships. For some women, however, retirement may symbolize the loss of a significant element of one's identity. This loss of identity may lead to a sense of dislocation that can place stress on a relationship. Being alert to how individual women and couples weather these changes and being willing to provide pastoral support and counsel in the midst of life transitions are important dimensions of tending lesbian relationships.

Renewal of Marriage

When I sat down at the table with Rose and Jim, I thought something seemed different. There was a warmth and affection between them that seemed more intense than I remembered. At first I thought that perhaps it was just a result of retirement and the release from the worries of the workaday world, but as the conversation continued it became clear that something more than that had changed between them. I had always seen their marriage as a positive one, with genuine respect and mutual regard for each other, but now there was an added dimension, a real joy in each other's presence. I learned that this was not just the result of retirement, but also the consequence of intentional work and a deepening intimacy.

Rose and Jim: Rediscovering Romance

Rose (discussed in chapter 4) is a seventy-year-old European American woman who has been married to Jim, seventy-four, for forty-six years. She and Jim have two adult children, one of whom is married with three children. Rose grew up in Virginia, graduated from high school in 1947, and then attended a large southern university, where she met her husband, although they did not date until after college. For three years after college, Rose taught school, primarily in the elementary grades. She continued to teach for a few years after she and Jim married in 1954. She grew up in a middle- to upper-middle-class home and continued in this same class and economic category after marriage.

Rose has worked on and off throughout her life, but her career was set aside while she was raising children. Jim's career as a Lutheran pastor took precedence and often determined where they would live. When her husband retired, he gave her the opportunity to select their retirement city. She chose a medium-size city in the south where they had lived previously and where her adult children now reside. She has old friends, including high school friends, in the community.

Jim's retirement was a significant transition for both of them. Jim suddenly had time and attention to devote to interests and concerns, including his marriage, which had received less attention during his working life. Rose also found her role changing significantly. Others' perception of her had been substantially tied to Jim's position. Now she was free to redefine herself in new ways.

Some of the activities that now shape Rose's life are her work with her church's refugee settlement committee, involvement with her grandchildren, learning new computer skills, e-mailing friends, reconnecting with old friends, and investing in her newly revitalized marriage.

DISCUSSION. A successful marriage can be defined in a number of ways, which may include both its duration and the level of satisfaction partners derive from the marriage. The majority of long-term married couples find marriage satisfying, although men report slightly higher levels of satisfaction with marriage than women do.[10] Research on long-term marriages discovered that marriages judged as successful were marked by friendship, enjoyment of one's spouse, commitment to the marriage, humor, and shared goals.[11] A sense of equity, or getting out of the marriage about as much as you put in, also seemed to affect the mood of the marital relationship.

From the outside, we typically judge a successful or satisfying marriage to be one that doesn't change much over time. According to family systems theory, however, a healthy marriage is marked by flexibility and adaptability of the marital bond over the course of the marriage. It is actually this flexibility and adaptability that provides stability. In addition to flexibility, marks of a healthy marriage include open communications, a well-defined sense of self for each partner, a relatively small power differential between partners, and a belief that the partner has one's best interest in mind.[12]

Family systems theory views marriage as a system in which the interactional patterns between partners affect individual behavior and individual behavior affects the marital system. The family system has two functions, which appear to be contradictory: (1) to maintain equilibrium or a certain degree of stability and (2) to adapt to developmental change.[13] Typical developmental changes in family life include the addition of children, the launching of children into adulthood, and retirement.[14] Any of such developmental changes can pose a crisis for a family or marriage unable to adapt to the systemic changes brought about by a new phase of life. Retirement can likewise represent an opportunity or a challenge to older couples, whose patterns of interacting may change significantly as a result of it. Rose and Jim found that retirement provided challenges but also ultimately an opportunity to deepen and renew their marital bond. It is this flexibility that typically keeps the bond strong.

Rose and Jim have been married forty-six years, having met in college, although they did not marry until a few years after graduating. Although Rose and Jim have each had their own careers, Jim's had taken prominence, and they moved often in response to it. Jim ended his career in a prominent position of leadership. Rose, though having dutifully followed Jim, had not always found the transitions easy. Recognizing this, Jim suggested to Rose that she should be the one to decide where they would retire. She chose a medium-size southern city where they had resided once before and where their children and grandchildren now live.

PASTORAL ASSESSMENT. Several times during the interview Rose commented on the renewal of her marriage and the positive difference this has made in her current enjoyment of retired life.

Rose: Change in the partner—it's just made all the difference in the world. We just get along so much better that it's almost a second honeymoon…We just do what we want to do…I feel like we've both just grown tremendously since retirement and since we have the time and freedom.

Retirement provided Jim and Rose the opportunity to deal with issues that had been set aside during the years of work and family. Freed from job-related role expectations, both Rose and Jim discovered dimensions of themselves that had been previously undeveloped. Sharing of these discoveries with each other eventually led to some intentional work on their marriage and to a deeper knowledge of one another.

Rose: But since retirement, he's even come and said, you know, what's wrong? Why did you say that like that? Which he'd never ever done before. So all that's been wonderful.

Interviewer. It sounds like sort of a second honeymoon.

Rose: It is. It is, you know—and rediscovering and appreciating each other in new ways.

Both Rose and Jim are clearly enjoying a renewed sense of emotional intimacy, something that, along with sexual intimacy, is still important to them. As we noted earlier, contrary to stereotypical assumptions about older adults, interest in sexuality continues over the life course for most older adults, and there is a positive correlation between marital satisfaction and sexual activity for older adults.[15] Much ignorance and prejudice remains about the sexual functioning and needs of older adults. Pastors can assist women and men in overcoming this ignorance and prejudice by educating themselves and others about sexuality. A perspective that does not limit sexuality to sexual activity but views it as an essential part of what it means to be human can lead to a greater appreciation of the role of sexuality across the life span.

Contrary to images of late-life marriage as a time of stagnation, or simply companionate relationship with little interest in sexual activity, Rose and Jim remind us that growth in one's intimate relationship can occur at any time over the life cycle. Retirement has provided Rose and Jim with the time and energy to devote to addressing issues in their marriage that were somewhat neglected earlier amid the commitments of career and family.

Although both Jim and Rose seemed to be enjoying the renewal of the marriage, it did seem to have a greater impact on Rose's sense of satisfaction and well-being at this point in her life. This observation is consistent with research indicating that the quality of the marital bond seems to have a greater impact on women's physical and mental health than men's, and that a positive experience of marriage had a larger impact on women's morale than men's.[16] Many women in the current cohort of older women were socialized to believe that marriage and family were their principal responsibilities and the primary vocation to which they should aspire. As a consequence, women may interpret the success or failure of a marriage as a personal failure or success.

Practices of Care

Tending the relationships of older married couples requires openness to the ongoing development that occurs in marriage. Caregivers need to be especially alert to life changes, such as retirement, and changes in health or residence that may present challenges to a couple. Although Rose and Jim experienced retirement as a time of marital renewal, for some couples retirement exposes underlying marital problems that could be avoided more easily when one or both spouses were working and had less time together. Pastors need to be reminded that older couples may want and need pastoral support and counseling late in life to deal with unresolved issues in a marriage or to deepen the sense of marital satisfaction. We must not assume that it is too late to make such changes or that attending to these issues will make little difference. Short-term pastoral counseling and revising the marital narrative may be enough to address these issues; if not, referral to a marital therapist is recommended.

Congregations can provide support and encouragement for married couples across the life span by providing educational courses that improve communication skills or that address issues of life transitions. Providing this kind of vocational discernment at retirement, as Sarah suggested in the previous chapter, can help couples anticipate relational changes that may accompany the end of a career. Helping couples imagine positive future stories through informal pastoral counseling or lay visitation may also improve their quality of life in the midst of changing life circumstances.

All three of the portraits we have viewed remind us that marriage and partnership are as important in late life as at any other life stage. They alert us to the variety of intimate relationships in late life and illustrate that these intimate relationships exist in a larger network of extended family relationships, friendships, and congregational contexts. Because these circles of relationships are interlocking, the support of families, friends, and congregations can certainly have a positive impact on an intimate relationship.

Older Women as Mothers and Grandmothers

Many, though not all, older women who are or have been married are also mothers and grandmothers. These roles are often an important part of the identity of older women, especially those age sixty and older, regardless of the age of their children. Women of these generations were socialized to expect motherhood to be their primary role. It is therefore no surprise that stories about children and grandchildren emerged spontaneously and held great importance in the interviews. For many women these relationships with adult children and grandchildren provide companionship and great pleasure in life, particularly now that they are freed from immediate caregiving responsibilities toward them. For example, Joan commented that her relationship with her great-grandchildren helps keep her young.

A desire to strengthen these bonds with progeny sometimes influences decisions such as where to live following retirement. Both Rose and Katherine made decisions about relocation influenced in part by a desire to be geographically closer to adult children and grandchildren in order to enjoy the companionship these relationships provide. Interdependence often marks these adult child relationships, because support and care are not simply provided by the younger generations to the older generations. For example, grandparents often provide help with child care and material support, and adult children provide companionship, support—such as help with household chores, shopping, or managing finances—and sometimes caregiving to older women. Older women often serve the role of "kin-keepers," maintaining ties across the generations of the family and on occasion serving as mediators between their children and grandchildren.[17]

As in any relationship, parents and children can experience times of conflict. Tending the relationships of older women will therefore also include an awareness of possible strains in the parent-child bond. Both communal support and short-term counseling are means of offering support in the midst of difficulties in the parent-child relationships. Friendship networks, established through church activities or other avenues, can be the source of much-needed encouragement when relationships with adult children are strained. Friends can provide support and encouragement to weather the difficult times. Katherine reports that her friends at church are an important source of support when her daughter seems to dismiss her advice. Hearing that her friends also have disagreements with their children, particularly over different values of childrearing, helps her realize that she is in good company. This awareness allows her to take differences of opinion less seriously, which results in her being less tense around her daughter.

At times, however, strains in the parent-child relationship become quite severe and can be the source of significant pain. Julie reminds us that the parent-child relationship is not always a positive one. She is estranged from her own son and lost her home in part due to conflict with her stepson. As a consequence, she cannot count on these relationships for support, and this has increased her sense of isolation and dependence on the church. Sometimes parents are not released from caregiving responsibilities, even when children reach adulthood. A worry for parents of developmentally disabled or chronically mentally ill children is the provision of care following the parent's death.

Whereas a mother may worry about how her children will fare after her death, surviving one's children is not often contemplated. The loss of a child at any age is difficult, not least because parents don't expect to outlive their children. Such a loss seems out of time. Jane, ninety-one, has been married and widowed twice and has lost both her children. Her son died in 1987 at age fifty, and her daughter died five years later at age fifty-two. Her daughter's death was particularly difficult because it followed so closely after her son's death and meant the loss of her only remaining child. She talks about this time in her life.

> When my daughter died, I just couldn't believe it. I knew she was going to die, but I was in denial. Although I knew she was going to die, she couldn't get well, I denied it. I thought, well, I can't make it after I lose her, I'll go too. I told my husband that. But after she died, that night, I know I didn't sleep any that night. I worried and I prayed all night. I thought, "What am I going to do? I just can't go on...I've already lost my son and now my daughter. I can't go on without my family, with both children gone and everything."

Jane found that her faith, her church, and her own sense of determination were essential to surviving her daughter's death.

> I told my husband the next morning, "I've just decided that I can spend the rest of my life grieving over Edith, and I'm tempted to do it because I am on that road. But I know it won't help her, it won't bring her back, and it won't help me. I'll die too because I can't live long in that kind of grief." I said, "I've decided to be thankful for the fifty-two years I

have had her and move on." And that is the decision I have made and that is what I have lived with. I felt real good after that because that is what I had to do, and that is what I did. I don't know if other people do it that way or not, but that was my way of doing it. I learned that you have to accept it and handle it the best you can. And that is what I have tried to do. And to me, it has worked. I can't say it would for other people because I know some other people who never come out of grief.

Although Jane has come out of her grief, the loss of her children is still a present memory. Jane has stayed connected with her son-in-law and her grandchildren. These relationships are a source of enjoyment in her life and allow her to stay connected to a part of her daughter's life. Jane's story illustrates that the death of a child is a powerful event, regardless of the age of the parent or child. We should not assume that because the child was grown the loss is less painful.

Tending the mother-child relationship includes an awareness of the sustaining power of this bond and that it continues to be important across the life span. At any point, this bond may be strained by conflict, be challenged by negotiating reciprocity and interdependence, or suffer the powerful blow of death. Because pastoral care requires careful assessment, we must stay attentive to developments in these relationships and provide support, counsel, and intervention when appropriate. Affirming the importance of this relationship acknowledges that a woman's life is composed of a mosaic of relationships.

Older Women's Friendships

In addition to siblings, parents, children, spouses or partners, and other extended family members, many women consider friends as a part of their extended family. All the fifteen women interviewed for this study mentioned the importance of friendship, and several named particular friends important to them. As noted previously, friendship ties may be particularly vital to single women. For many women, close friends have been the crucial factor in helping them move with strength and integrity through the transitions of widowhood, retirement, or relocation. Although long-term friendships seem to have significant meaning for many women, a number of the women who were relatively new residents at the retirement home where I conducted several interviews clearly had put significant effort into making new friends in their new settings. These friendships were often formed through other activities such as exercise classes, volunteering, or educational opportunities. Although research indicates that long-term friendships appear to have a higher degree of emotional closeness, for the women in my sample making friends in a new place was fundamental to a sense of belonging and well-being.[18]

Both Rose and Joan talked about their efforts to make new friends following relocation to a new home. Rose comments, "To make new friends at this stage is hard." Rose formed new friendships by finding new activities, such as volunteering to work with a refugee family in her church. She also connected with old friends by volunteering for a fiftieth high school reunion. Joan also reports that it has been through her volunteer activities that she has made new friends. Clearly these friendships are important to older women, and they invest time in making and maintaining them. For Joan, her women friends are confidants and supporters with whom she could share her struggles when the demands of caregiving were overwhelming. This sense of having the listening ear of someone with similar life experience, along with a sense of reciprocity, are common elements of women's friendships.[19]

Not surprisingly, many older women noted that their friends were often close to their own age, for although many women mentioned that they enjoyed friendships with younger women, it was often with younger women that older women felt most invisible. Several of the experiences of invisibility reported in earlier chapters involved interactions between women of differing generations. At least five of the women interviewed indicated a sense of often being ignored or seen as irrelevant by younger women. This was puzzling and troubling for them, and they often expressed a desire for better relationships with younger women.

Both the importance of women's friendships and this particular issue of strain between older and younger women raise significant questions for pastoral care and congregational ministry with older women. How might congregations provide opportunities for older women to expand their friendship networks, which are often an important source of support? How might the church foster better intergenerational relationships between older and younger women in the congregation so that each might be a source of support for the other? Intentionally fostering and tending older women's friendships is one means through which congregations can become good places for women to grow old.

Congregations guided by a vision of the church as a place of gracious inclusion recognize the relational character and context of our lives. These relationships with partners, children, friends, and other family members change and grow over time, sometimes giving pleasure and sometimes causing pain. As with any other living, growing thing, relationships need tending, nurture, and care. Relational practices of care are a means of honoring interdependence as essential to our humanity.

Yet on occasion, relationships wound us and narratives harm us. At such times, it is the responsibility of the church to work for justice and liberation. We now turn to prophetic practices of care, which are often called for at moments of relational and narrative failure.

CHAPTER 7

Prophetic Practices of Care

As Betty speaks, I am transported to the Apollo Theater in New York City. It is 1932; Duke Ellington is playing, and Betty is on stage twirling and kicking as a dancer in the chorus. Betty's eyes sparkle as she recounts the story of this high time in her life. She still imagines returning to New York to live on her own once again. I look around me. It is the year 2000; we are not at the Apollo but in a sunny room filled with vinyl chairs and plastic plants and many other older women. This is where Betty, eighty-eight, comes during the day while her daughter, her caretaker, is working. It is a county day-care program for older adults. Now, wheelchair bound and missing a leg from complications of diabetes and gangrene, Betty still dreams of dancing.

Betty, who struggles with a number of health problems and would face poverty without the assistance of her daughter, reminds us that late life can be a difficult time for some older women. Most of the stories we have encountered so far have been of relatively healthy women living independently, either in their own homes or a senior residence. Although three of the women interviewed are living on quite limited incomes, they are still able to live on their own, through the support of Social Security, Medicare, and other programs. Late life can be a time of personal and spiritual growth, even in the midst of health challenges for many. But for some, like Betty, an African American woman, the lifetime effects of poverty and discrimination can impact health, which in turn affects the overall quality of later life. Research into the relationship between socioeconomic status and health shows a high correlation between poverty and chronic illness, disability, and death.[1]

Betty's daughter, who is in her early sixties, is still working and providing care for her mother. As she has found, these burdens of caregiving fall disproportionately on women, and as is the case here, a younger older woman is often caring for an older relative. The strains of caregiving can also negatively impact the health of women and on occasion lead to elder abuse. Betty is fortunate that this is not the case, but evidence of strains in the mother-daughter relationship does surface in the interview.

The hardship of poverty, the burden of caregiving, and the tragedy of abuse present in the lives of some older women call us to practices of prophetic witness. Through prophetic witness we challenge oppressive social practices, which diminish the quality of life for older women. Such witness is often necessary when social narratives diminish rather than affirm the worth of persons and interpersonal and family relationships wound rather than nurture. Prophetic practices may intersect with both narrative and relational practices.

Prophetic practices of care are rooted in the biblical imperative to care for the widowed and oppressed, those for whom God advocates. This in turn lays the responsibility at our feet to pay particular attention to those least able to fend for themselves. Prophetic practices of care include advocacy, affirming narratives of resistance, and critiquing the cultural narratives of aging in light of the vision of gracious inclusion of the Christian story. We begin our discussion of prophetic practices with advocacy.

Advocacy

An advocate is one who speaks on behalf of another, usually one who does not have much public "voice," but advocacy also spills over into action taken on behalf of another. Advocacy is needed in situations of oppression, marginalization, or violence. It includes addressing systemic issues of justice implicit in particular situations of care, such as redressing the imbalance of income between men and women, or finding ways to financially compensate women for their labors in childrearing and caregiving, important social tasks that are not merely private. Social attitudes that render older women less visible also often render them not credible, not believed, and as a result increasingly unwilling or unable to vocalize their needs. Women seventy and older come from generations of women who were generally not encouraged to speak up, and they have become habituated to being silent about their own needs.

As advocates for older women, congregations can become informed about the issues facing older women, acknowledge the way attitudes toward aging can affect social policy, and work through political processes to ensure the development of social programs and policies that promote the well-being of older women. Many women face *economic insecurity,* due to lifelong patterns of exploitation and marginalization in the workforce. *Abuse in late life* is a problem that is often not recognized and can place women at great risk.

Caregiving, a responsibility that many older women increasingly take on, often exacts both a physical, mental, and financial toll on women. Inadequate financial and community resources available to assist women in this task only increase the burden. Pastoral advocacy in these situations may include both intervention in a particular situation and addressing the larger systemic conditions that underlie the individual case. We move now to a discussion of these three issues and advocacy as an expression of prophetic witness and care.[2]

Economic Security

Over the past three decades, the economic status of older adults as a group has improved substantially. The general perception is that older adults are well off. As the population ages, the specter of an ever-increasing, wealthy "gray lobby" demanding more and more social benefits at the expense of other groups, such as children, is often offered as political justification to reduce spending on Social Security or Medicare. The accuracy of such a depiction of the aging population is rarely questioned, but it should be.

On the surface the income picture for older adults as a whole looks good; the overall poverty rates for older adults were at a historic low in 1999. When we look below the surface and beyond aggregate figures for income, the picture becomes more complex. Although the overall poverty rates for older adults dropped to a low of 9.7 percent in 1999, these rates are not evenly divided among the population. Almost three quarters of all older persons with incomes below the poverty level are women.[3] A number of organizations that advocate for older women, including the U.S. Administration on Aging, the Older Women's League, and the American Association of Retired Persons, have identified economic security as one of the primary challenges facing older women.

For some older women, poverty is a lifelong condition, whereas for others poverty accompanies widowhood, retirement, or divorce. Because only about half of elderly women receive pension income, many older women are dependent on Social Security.[4] Women over the age of sixty-five comprise 60 percent of Social Security beneficiaries, and women over eighty-five represent 72 percent of recipients. Slightly more than one quarter (27 percent) rely on Social Security for 90 percent of their retirement income. Social Security benefits are often insufficient, leaving women at greater and increasing risk of impoverishment when compared with men as they age.

Social Security was designed to be gender neutral. Men and women who work for the same number of years at the same pay should receive the same benefits when they retire. In practice, however, relatively few women draw the same benefits as men. For most women, the experiences of life are not gender neutral, and they work for fewer years at lower wages than men and inevitably draw smaller retirement benefits. Policy changes reducing Social Security benefits or increasing the retirement age will most likely have the greatest impact on women, who are the most dependent on these programs.

Minority women, and single women regardless of race, are particularly vulnerable to poverty. The poverty rate for single women is 21 percent. More than half of all women over the age of sixty-five are single, and the majority of these women are widowed. More than half the elderly widows living in poverty were not poor before their husband's death.[5] Divorced women often fare worse economically than widowed women, and African American widows and single Hispanic women are among the poorest and most vulnerable older women.[6] Older poor women have often been full-time homemakers whose income was largely contingent on a former husband's earning, had work histories in low-paying jobs, or had histories of "seasonal, interrupted or marginal work."[7]

Betty, who still dreams of dancing, experiences poverty due to discrimination in the workplace as an African American woman who had limited access to jobs with benefits. It is unlikely that her job at the Apollo Theater paid Social Security benefits. Like many older women in poverty, Betty worked lower-paying marginal jobs much of her life and interrupted her work history to care for her family. Her husband's death in 1970 further increased her economic insecurity.

Julie, whom we met in chapter 3, was also pushed into poverty following her (second) husband's death. Like many older women, Julie had not been consistently in the workforce, interrupting her working life to care for her children and later her second husband as he was dying of cancer. She was primarily dependent on her husband's income. Although she brought a small amount of equity from the home acquired in her first marriage, she was quite vulnerable economically. She combined her small resources with her second husband, only to lose these upon his death. Julie is fortunate in that when she confided in her minister, he was knowledgeable about available resources and able to connect her with these.

Practicing Advocacy: From Economic Insecurity to Security

Responding to individual situations such as Julie's, however, does not address the larger systemic factors that put women at jeopardy.

Pastors and congregations can be advocates for older woman by educating themselves about relevant economic issues facing older women and by promoting beneficial public policies. Economic advocacy requires an awareness of the economic challenges facing older women in their individual lives and as a group. On the individual level, awareness means knowing that when a woman is widowed or divorced late in life, she is likely to experience a significant drop in income. On the public policy level, awareness includes a willingness to examine public policies and programs such as Social Security that disproportionately affect the financial security of older women.

Addressing the challenge of economic insecurity on the individual level includes empowering older women—and women in general—to be knowledgeable about and in control of their finances. Education can thus also be a form of advocacy. Educational programs that help older women prepare for retirement and increase their knowledge of financial issues may not change a woman's income, but such programs may help her manage limited resources more effectively. Many women now in their seventies and older were raised to believe that financial matters were primarily a husband's responsibility. Although many couples readily share information about finances, some women find themselves having to quickly master new skills in managing money following a husband's illness or their own widowhood or divorce. Women who have never in their lives balanced a checkbook, prepared their income taxes, or set up a household budget might welcome some rather basic and patient assistance in developing these skills. Other women with adequate resources for retirement may be at risk of losing them to unscrupulous advisers if these women are not educated about how to manage these resources.

Providing such financial education for older women can occur in many ways. In larger congregations, short-term courses can be offered as part of the larger educational program or women's societies might make this information available to their members. Although pastors may not be expert in these financial affairs, lay members in congregations often are. In smaller churches, such education can occur on a more informal basis by matching older women with others who might provide basic education about investing and financial matters or advice on how to select a financial adviser.

Being knowledgeable about resources available in the larger community and connecting older women to these is also a form of advocacy as an expression of care. Congregations can link women with organizations knowledgeable about benefits and resources available to assist older women, such as the Older Women's League, the Women's Institute for a Secure Retirement, or the American

Association for Retired Persons.[8] All these organizations provide basic information and resources. According to AARP, many of the older adults eligible for financial assistance programs such as Supplemental Social Security Income, Medicaid, or food stamps are not aware of these programs. Most counties have a department or commission on aging responsible for coordinating services for older adults. By linking eligible women with these programs, we can often improve their quality of life. One good way to do this might be to have literature on such programs available at the church.

Churches can be advocates for older women by combining awareness with lobbying for public policies that will improve their economic security. This means not only addressing the programs that directly affect older women but also redressing the economic inequalities over the course of a woman's life that put her at greater risk for poverty in late life. The underlying issues of income parity must be addressed.[9] To achieve such parity, solutions to disrupted job tenure must be found and greater returns on educational achievements must be achieved.[10] The economic status of future cohorts of older women depends on changes in the economic status and employment situation for women in general and throughout their lifetimes.[11]

Poverty in late life is not simply a matter of poor individual decisions, but reflects a culturally constructed narrative that devalues women's work, blocks equity in the workplace, and influences social policies. Narrative reconstruction, which occurs at the individual level and social level, leads not only to new interpretations but also to enactments of these reconstructed narratives through congregational practices and public policy.

Violence and Abuse in Late Life

Just as social narratives and practices can constrain and diminish the quality of women's lives, so too can women's central relationships harm rather than heal. When relationships with spouses or adult children become abusive, older women are put at risk of injury or death. Violence and abuse, in whatever form they appear, are no respecters of age. This reality calls us to attend to the potential for violence across the life span.

Older women potentially face abuse in various forms, including physical and sexual violence, neglect, and financial exploitation. Our discussion focuses on three forms of abuse most common to older women: *domestic violence*, which occurs between partners; *elder abuse*, which refers to the mistreatment or neglect of an older person by a caregiver; and *sexual abuse*, which can accompany both domestic violence and elder abuse. To respond to violence against older women, we need to understand its contours. We begin by exploring domestic violence in late life.

Domestic violence, or *woman battering,* is a form of behavior that establishes control in a relationship.[12] Battering is not just about individual instances of violence but is typically a pattern of behavior. Such domestic violence includes threats; psychological abuse; injuring or killing of pets; controlling a woman's activities; physical violence such as kicking, punching, and slapping; sexual humiliation; and rape.[13] Battering is life threatening; any single attack can result in serious injury or death.[14]

Domestic violence "grown old" occurs when violence that started earlier in life continues into old age.[15] In such cases, abuse has become a long-term pattern in the marriage. Women who have grown up in violent homes and have never lived away from partners, spouses, or families of origin may know no other life. Violence may be accepted as one of those things one has to endure. The long-term effects of battering can lead to the loss of a woman's sense of reality as it is replaced by the abuser's interpretation of reality. This may reduce her ability to evaluate the danger she is in or to realize that another way of life is possible. A woman in a long-term abusive relationship may lose confidence in her ability to live apart from her partner and to support herself financially. Although some marriages are plagued from the start with violence, it is not unusual for changes in circumstance to precipitate late-onset domestic violence in long-standing relationships that have not previously been violent. In marriages that are already highly conflicted, changes such as retirement, ill health, or other stressful life events can be triggers for late-onset violence. The increased chaos introduced by the life event one cannot change or control may lead a husband to behave abusively toward his wife, whom he can control. In some cases, violence can be a symptom of an illness, such as Alzheimer's disease or some forms of mental illness.

Some older women experiencing violence may have been in previously nonviolent relationships and experience violence when starting a new relationship in late life. These women may have difficulty acknowledging the violence and may not think of themselves as abused. Because images of abused women are often of younger women with children, older women may be left with the impression that violence does not occur in late life, leading them to minimize the violence that is occurring.

Older women may find it more difficult to leave an abusive partner for a number of reasons, including the effects of long-term battering. The real financial insecurity that faces older women may also influence their decision to stay. As previously noted, older women who have not been in the workforce consistently and may not have pension or Social Security benefits of their own are often financially dependent on the husbands' income. Age discrimination in the workplace makes it difficult to find work with adequate pay that allows financial self-sufficiency. In addition to these factors, the abusive situation itself may increase the precariousness of a woman's financial situation. One form of control that abusers use is financial, which can take the form of restricting a woman's access to money, controlling family finances, or prohibiting work outside the home. Women who are past retirement age, have been prevented from outside work, and are not eligible for Social Security apart from a husband's income are likely to feel financially trapped in the abusive relationship. In addition, some older women may fear the anticipated consequences of intervention, such as losing their homes, being placed in nursing homes, or being declared incompetent to care for themselves.

Older women are not only at risk of being abused by partners but also can be abused by adult children or caregivers. Abuse perpetrated either by a caregiver or a relative other than a spouse is identified as elder abuse.[16] *Elder abuse* is a broad term that includes physical abuse, "the non-accidental infliction of pain or injury," psychological abuse, the "affliction of mental anguish," material abuse, financial exploitation, neglect, and intentional or unintentional "refusal to provide adequate care."[17] About two thirds of the victims of elder abuse are women, according to 1996 statistics. This may be due in part to the demographic realities of late life; older women simply outnumber men. Elder abuse most often occurs to women who are ill, handicapped, or have other conditions that make them dependent on others for care, such as dementia or developmental disabilities. Older women also have higher rates of chronic and handicapping conditions than do men, which may also explain their increased risk for abuse.

Elder abuse might occur for a number of reasons; one common factor contributing to abuse is caregiver stress. Family members or paid caregivers attending to persons with dementia may be particularly susceptible to caregiver stress that might lead to abuse, particularly neglect, which is the most common form of abuse. Persons with advanced dementia, including Alzheimer's disease, need twenty-four-hour-a-day care. These persons may be incontinent, unable to feed themselves, severely disoriented, and prone to wander if not in a secure environment. This kind of care is extremely taxing, particularly for older caregivers or those with multiple caregiving and work responsibilities. Caregivers who would not normally be abusive or neglectful might become so in response to the overwhelming demands of caregiving in such a situation.

Long-standing patterns of family interactions also contribute to the likelihood of elder abuse. In families in which violence has shaped patterns of relating between parents and children, elder abuse may be both an extension of and reversal of this abuse. This may explain why adult children are the most common perpetrators of elder abuse. Adult children, who suffer from chronic mental illness or substance abuse and experience violence related to these conditions, are also more prone to be abusive. The risk of abuse increases when an older parent is forced to live with an abusive child due to restricted finances. Patterns of family interaction in which adult children are overly dependent on the victimized senior for financial assistance also increase the risk of abuse. The abuse may be an attempt to coerce the victim into relinquishing control of the finances.[18]

One form of elder abuse that receives little attention is *sexual abuse.* On some occasions, caretakers, including adult children, sexually abuse older women. In a 1991 study of cases of elder abuse accompanied by sexual abuse, the offenders were usually relatives of victims. The most common form of abuse in this study was vaginal rape.[19] Victims who are dependent on these family members for care may be reluctant to report the abuse. Shame and privacy about sexual matters may also reduce the likelihood that older women will report sexual abuse.

Advocacy in Situations of Abuse

Congregations can be advocates for abused older women by breaking the silence. Acknowledging the reality of violence in women's lives regardless of age, education, or economic situations is an important first step. Moving from awareness to action includes a willingness to speak openly on behalf of women and to hold abusers accountable. As the church becomes less silent about the issue of domestic violence and elder abuse, victims will feel freer to bring this issue to the attention of clergy. We must make it quite clear that such violence against women is contrary to Christian teaching.[20]

Congregational caregivers, both pastoral and laity, need to be knowledgeable about the resources for older women available in the community. Referral to domestic violence programs can interrupt situations of domestic violence and ensure the safety of the victim, the first step in intervention. Congregations with ongoing relationships to domestic violence shelters can work with these shelters to offer counseling and other services that meet the needs of older women. For example, congregations partnering with shelters might help educate shelter volunteers about the increased economic vulnerability of older women and the availability of state and local services specifically for such women. Shelters might also provide emergency clothing in a variety of sizes and styles or written materials in large print, which might demonstrate sensitivity to the needs of older women.

Advocacy around issues of elder abuse also begins with awareness and breaking the silence. This includes acknowledging that situations of elder abuse might be occurring in one's own congregation. Because elder abuse often occurs when older women are frail or in ill health, pastors and laity visiting members who are homebound need to be attentive for possible signs of abuse. Lay visitors can be trained to assess for indications of abuse or potential abuse, such as severe caregiver stress. Signs of violence might include inordinate control of the visit by a spouse or caregiver, prohibiting subsequent visits, or signs of physical abuse, including suspicious bruising or broken bones. When a lay visitor suspects such violence, a referral should be made to the pastor or, in the case of elder abuse, to adult protective services. Because elder abuse can occur in institutional settings, as well as the home, pastors or laity visiting church members in nursing homes should also be attentive to signs of abuse. Most states have agencies that regulate nursing homes and intervene in cases of institutional elder abuse.

Sexual abuse is probably the most underreported form of abuse among older women, who may be reluctant to talk to a pastor or pastoral caregiver about these issues because of feelings of self-blame, shame, or fear of moral judgment. Creating an atmosphere of trust is vitally important if women are to reveal these issues. Because sexual abuse usually accompanies domestic violence or elder abuse, intervention in these cases may address the issue. Working with other trained caregivers, such as adult protective services in cases of elder abuse, rape crisis centers, or domestic violence shelters, can provide important support and resources to pastors, parish nurses, or lay caregivers who suspect such abuse.

Because elder abuse can be the result of severe caregiver stress, referral to county or state-sponsored senior programs that offer respite care and other assistance to family caregivers may reduce the possibility of future abuse in some cases. Associating abuse with caregiving highlights the need for attention to this crucial issue. As the population ages, the need for caregiving will increase and we will see more older women caring for ill spouses or elderly parents. Centenarians are now one of the fastest growing segments of the population. Assuming they don't outlive their children, we are likely to see women in their seventies and eighties caring for the oldest among us.[21]

Caregiving

Families, not institutions, provide most of the long-term care for older adults in the United States, and three quarters of family caregivers of older adults are women. Caregiving is thus largely a women's issue. As such it demands our attention as we seek to care effectively for older women.[22] The role of caregiver is one in which older women are increasingly finding themselves in late life. As of 1997, 82 percent of the family caregivers for chronically ill elders were women.[23] Sixty percent of caregivers are wives caring for husbands who are ill. Of these 60 percent, 73 percent are women over the age of sixty-five.[24]

Both Joan and Kate, whom we got to know in chapter 5, became caregivers in late life. Although both Kate and Joan are retired, Betty's daughter, who is in her early sixties, is still working. A large-scale study on women and caregiving found that not only does caregiving become an increasingly likely role for women as they age but more women are combining paid work and caregiving.[25] This is particularly true for women with lower incomes, who lack the resources for paid help to care for aging family members.

Caregiving can exact a heavy toll on older women. Women in this role often face isolation because they are unable to leave an ill or frail relative alone for any length of time. This social isolation increases physical and emotional stress, putting a woman at greater risk for developing physical or psychological problems.[26] Advocacy for women in this role is an appropriate and necessary response, because of the potentially negative impact that caregiving can have on a woman's life and health. [27]

The experience of caregiving can range from the provision of general support for a frail but generally healthy older adult to twenty-four-hour-a-day care for a seriously ill family member. Kate's experience is an example of the care required for a frail but generally healthy older woman of advanced age. Iris, Kate's mother, remained in relatively good health until age ninety-seven, though her excursions out of the house became quite limited when she reached her nineties. Kate and Iris provided mutual companionship for each other, and Kate did most of the cooking and household chores. Even though Iris was relatively healthy, she might not have been able to remain in her home without Kate's presence. As Iris became older, Kate did find she had to limit her activities away from the home, which made it more difficult for her to maintain her own friendships and network of social support.

Joan was also cast into the caregiver role in her seventies. She provided care for her husband, who was seriously ill the last few years of his life. Their move to a senior residence was due in large part to her recognition that she needed a more supportive environment as her husband's health worsened. Even when released from the task of preparing all the daily meals, the demands of caregiving caused some strain in her relationship with her husband. Joan's husband had a number of physical ailments, including diabetic neuropathy, high blood pressure, and the beginning signs of Alzheimer's disease. Joan comments on some of the demands of her role and the impact of her husband's illness on their relationship.

> It's been a challenge, of course; he had a lot of health problems before he died. I had to prepare his medications, except for insulin; he was always able to give himself insulin. But he had so many pills and so I had to do that weekly; I got them ready for him. I always had to help him button his shirts and tie his shoes. You know, he would just call on me for so many things. And sometimes of course, he was irritable, and I was irritable back. It was just sometimes more than we could stand.

Joan also indicates that she experienced some health-related problems due to the physical and emotional demands of caregiving, a role that she willingly fulfilled. In addition to physical problems such as stomach aches and back pain, caregivers are also prone to depression as a consequence of feeling the pressure of being the sole provider for a relative's needs.[28]

Despite the demands of caregiving, some women do experience positive benefits. For example, 36 percent of respondents to the National Family Caregivers Association survey reported developing a closer relationship with the person for whom they were caring. A number of caregivers found a new sense of competency and became aware of inner strengths that helped them face the challenges of caregiving.[29] The possibility of this occurrence may depend on the extent of the demands, the caregiver's health, and the resources available for support in this role.

Congregational Strategies for Care

As the population continues to age, the need for family caregiving for older adults will increase, and as we have seen, the burden will fall primarily on older women. Congregations can be advocates for their older female members who are in this role in at least three ways: by being informed about the demands of care; by providing concrete support for caregivers, such as respite care; and by supporting public policies and legislation that increases services for caregivers. We will look at each of these expressions of advocacy in turn.

Becoming informed about caregiving issues happens at two levels. Congregations can learn about the general needs of caregivers through a number of sources. The U.S. Administration on Aging maintains a website that provides detailed and current information on statistics and available services. In addition, this agency maintains a toll-free number, the Elder Care Locator (1-800-677-1116), a service linking caregivers to resources in their communities. The National Family Caregivers Association also maintains a Web site, www.nfcacares.org, that provides both general information and links to resources for support.

In addition to being informed on the general level, congregations need to be informed about the specific situations in the lives of their members. Clergy and lay members making home visits can be attentive to signs of caregiver stress. Taking the initiative to ask caregivers how they are doing communicates a sense that the caregiver is not alone in this task. A careful assessment of the caregiving situation is needed to determine if outside assistance, such as a visiting nurse or respite care, would be beneficial. Parish nurses might perform this assessment in a congregation. Most cities and counties have personnel in their departments on aging that can assist congregations in this task.

Once congregational care providers become aware of concrete needs in particular situations, strategies can be devised to meet some of these needs. Specific acts of care include home visits and short-term respite care. A visitor can give both the care receiver and caregiver a break by providing an alternative conversation partner. For example, when I visited Kate and Iris I provided a set of fresh ears for stories that Kate had heard many times. Being new to the city, I was glad to hear Iris's observations on how things had changed since she was a child. In situations of illness, a visitor can also bring a bit of normalcy into the situation, taking the focus off the illness for a time. A conversation about baseball, fishing, gardening, or politics might be a welcome change from discussing medicines or the scheduling of the next chemotherapy treatment. These tasks of managing treatment often fall to the caregiver and may be much of the focus of conversation on a day-to-day basis.

Short-term respite care, which allows a caregiver to go to a doctor's appointment, go shopping, or just have a little time alone, usually does not require significant training and can be provided by members of the congregation. Linking caregivers to community services can also be an important form of care. Caregivers overwhelmed with the task at hand may not be aware of the resources available or have the time to investigate various options. Narrative practices of care may support this process of linking caregiver with resources by helping a caregiver challenge the assumption that accepting assistance is a relinquishment of her responsibilities as a caregiver. Such narrative intervention may become increasingly important at the point at which care can no longer be safely provided in the home, as in the care of advanced Alzheimer's disease, when wandering behavior puts the ill person at risk.

Through joining forces with organizations such as the National Family Caregivers Association or the Older Women's League, congregations can help work toward legislation that improves services and support for caregivers. An example of legislation that is beneficial to care providers is the Family Medical Leave Act of 1993, which is intended to ensure that businesses address, among other issues, the needs of employees with regard to elder care. Also, the Older Americans Act Amendments of 2000 established new programs on family caregiving under the guidance of the Administration on Aging and the U.S. Department of Health and Human Services. Pastors and lay caregivers can support the enactment of this type of legislation and, by being knowledgeable about such programs, can assist caregivers in applying for available benefits such as family medical leave.

Because caregiving is often associated with illness and may precede the death of one of the partners, as it did in Joan's case, pastoral care may also take the form of assisting family members in preparing for death. Such care might include both the permission to talk about the possibility of death and planning a funeral or other services. Several women in the interview study emphasized the importance of caring for one's survivors by planning for one's own death, which meant getting financial and legal affairs in order, making clear the disposition of one's possessions, and planning for the funeral. All the women who made these suggestions had been involved in the death of relatives where this had not been the case. Katherine, who cared for her aunt during her final illness, was overwhelmed with details following the funeral.

> But when it was over, when the illness was over, I was faced with this two-story house to dismantle, and going through all the subsequent paying of the bills—and this and that and the other, going through her personal stuff—I was just about at wits end. Because of the experience, I don't want my children to have to disrupt their entire life [at my death]. And I have made a practice in the past five years to organize my affairs so that it won't create the pain that I went through. Family members are reluctant to discuss these issues. But I decided I did not want to ignore these issues. It is important to ask: What do you want after you're gone?

In situations where family members are reluctant to raise these issues, pastoral caregivers can take the initiative to begin such a discussion. Family members usually see the liturgical leadership for end of life rituals as a legitimate part of a pastor's role, and they may be less resistant to such a conversation with a clergy person for that reason.

Advocacy can take many forms and can include giving voice to women who have none, as well as acts of care that improve the lives of women facing economic insecurity, abuse, or the burdens of caregiving. Pastoral advocacy in these situations may include both intervening in a particular situation and addressing the larger systemic conditions that underlie the individual case. Because advocacy is about giving voice, narrative practices of care often accompany and support prophetic practices.

Narrative and prophetic practices intertwine in a variety of ways. In some instances, prophetic practices of care are needed when social narratives diminish older women or family narratives constrain older women's lives. In other cases, narrative practices support prophetic practices by providing a reinterpretation of a situation that leads to more liberating choices. For example, a woman might refuse assistance in caring for her ill husband for fear that she will be seen as abandoning her husband's care to strangers. A narrative reinterpretation might help her accept a congregation's concrete acts of support, such as respite care, which are an expression of the congregation's ministry of advocacy and prophetic witness.

Prophetic Narrative Practices

Narrative practices intersect with prophetic practice at several points. One point of intersection, just mentioned, is that in which larger social narratives confine or constrain a personal narrative. A second point of intersection occurs when women articulate narratives of resistance, as Sarah did when she objected to being overlooked for leadership positions following her retirement. Narratives of resistance enable women to retain a positive self-definition over against cultural definitions. The third point of connection occurs in the ongoing process of juxtaposing social narratives of aging and older women with the Christian narrative as it calls us to a vision of gracious inclusion, reminding us that late life can be a time of growth and renewal, as is evident in Rose's story, and not just a period of decline. We turn now to a further examination of these intersections of narrative practice and prophetic witness.

Challenging Confining Social Narratives

Returning to Betty's case, we can see how confining social narratives impact her life. Social narratives about Betty's diminished worth as an African American woman were enacted through practices that restricted her access to work with adequate pay and through other forms of overt and covert discrimination. As a result of lifelong discrimination, Betty now faces poverty and ill health in her later years. As noted earlier, there is a strong correlation between poverty and ill health in late life. Betty probably had little access to health care that might have prevented the loss of her leg.

As a consequence of her ill health and limited income, Betty is no longer able to live on her own and is now dependent on her daughter both financially and for her care. This situation of dependency is clearly difficult for Betty and was expressed in her desire to return to New York to live on her own, though it was no longer possible. In the face of a difficult situation, she returned to an idealized vision of the past and was unable to construct a narrative that allowed her to see her current situation in a positive light. Betty seems to understand her daughter's intervention as interference and control rather than care. However, according to the staff at the day program that Betty attended, her daughter appeared to be her mother's strong advocate and was petitioning the county for additional services for her mother.

Betty's interpretation of her current situation as confinement and constriction has led to friction with her daughter. This interpretation may be due in part to a strong narrative of independence that has always been a part of Betty's self-understanding. In her current situation, this narrative is severely challenged, yet she seeks to maintain it even in the face of opposing evidence. Pastoral intervention that helps Betty reinterpret her situation and offers her a working model of interdependence might ease some of the friction between Betty and her daughter. It is also important that the pastoral care provider affirm that the situation that Betty and her daughter face is not entirely of their own making. Larger social forces have been at work constructing many elements of their current situation. Narrative practices of care that help Betty shape a more constructive narrative of the present and future, along with relational practices that support Betty and her daughter, complement prophetic practices that address the larger systemic issues underlying the situations that Betty and her daughter face.

Narratives of Resistance

Narrative practices of care also intersect with prophetic practices of care when we affirm narratives of resistance. By constructing a narrative of resistance, an older woman claims the authority to tell her own life story and refuses social definition that diminishes her or renders her invisible. Evidence of narratives of resistance was evident throughout the interviews. One such embodied narrative of resistance is evident in Ann's defiant act of juggling, which immediately redefines her from an invisible older woman to a very visible one.

The most common form of this narrative was the rejection of chronology as defining old age. Because *old* is not simply a descriptive term but is value laden, with connotations of senility and decline, most of the women rejected this definition. This resistance to being defined as old was evident in Joan's narrative, as we saw in chapter 2. Joan consistently asserted that she did not feel old and that she was not old, according to the definition of old as "inactive and uninterested in life." Kate gives voice to a similar narrative of resistance when asked what advice she might give young pastors.

> Forget age. That is not important. Don't focus on a number. It doesn't tell you anything. Ask about their interests and activities. As soon as you pin down a number, you limit people. We have got to erase the idea that age makes a difference.

Kate, Joan, and Ann were aware that they were in late life. This became quite evident in the responses to the question about how life had changed over the past twenty years. Each of these women named both new challenges and opportunities that accompanied aging. None of them was unrealistic about her situation. Each of these women, however, refused to be defined simply in terms of social meanings of older women.

Part of our prophetic work occurs when we hear and affirm these narratives of resistance. At times we may need to help a woman articulate such a narrative. Katherine, for example, wants to be seen in her fullness as a person and not be restricted to the stereotypical image of grandmother. Through the intersection of prophetic and narrative practices, we might both nurture her narrative of resistance through conversation and affirm this narrative through congregational practices that allow her to express her variety of gifts in the life of the congregation.

Our ability to hear and affirm these narratives of resistance is dependent on our ability to question the accepted social construction of age and stereotypical images of older women. Such questioning occurs when we intentionally evaluate the dominant social narratives in light of the Christian narrative and its vision of gracious inclusion.

Toward a Narrative of Gracious Inclusion

Narrative practices of care further intersect with prophetic practices as we continually juxtapose the Christian narrative and its vision of gracious inclusion with our social practices toward older women. This juxtaposition calls us to the ongoing practice of self-examination and repentance. The Christian narrative also moves us to embrace a theological vision of aging, in which late life is seen as a time of spiritual and emotional growth, as well as time of loss. A theological vision of aging also affirms the relational character of human life and that our own growth and fulfillment is inextricably linked to others. We must continually ask ourselves if our practices of care in this congregation embrace the full experience of aging. Do we encourage and assist women in vocational discernment so that new and fitting forms of discipleship may be discovered at each stage of life?

A vision of the church as a place of gracious inclusion beckons us toward a community in which neither age, gender, ability, nor ethnicity determines one's worth. Such a community is rooted in the life of the triune God, which calls it into being. Enabled by God's grace, we embody this vision of the church through concrete practices of care. As we embody narrative, relational, and prophetic practices of care, we respond to God's gracious initiative.

Narrative practices enable the collaborative process of telling stories in which the worth and dignity of older women are affirmed. By encouraging narratives of resistance, we assist older women in revising social constructions of age that diminish them. Relational practices acknowledge the reality of our lives as intimately connected to one another. Through these practices we support and strengthen the networks of older women that nourish and sustain them, and we intervene when these relationships harm rather than heal. Prophetic practices proclaim our commitment to embodying justice and resisting oppression. Through these practices we become advocates for older women. As we weave these three practices of care together, we fashion a fabric of ecclesial life in which older women can flourish.

Selected Bibliography

Anderson, H., and Foley, E. *Mighty Stories, Dangerous Rituals: Weaving Together the Human and Divine.* San Francisco: Jossey-Bass, 1998.

Atchley, R. C. *Continuity and Adaptation in Aging: Creating Positive Experiences.* Baltimore: Johns Hopkins University Press, 1999.

Arber, S., and Ginn, J. *Gender and Later Life: A Sociological Analysis of Resources and Constraints.* London: Sage Publications, 1991.

Black, H. K. R. Rubenstein. *Old Souls: Aged Women, Poverty, and the Experience of God.* New York: Aldine De Gruyter, 2000.

Browning, D. S. *A Fundamental Practical Theology: Descriptive and Strategic Proposals.* Minneapolis: Fortress Press, 1991.

Chopp, R. *Saving Work: Feminist Practices of Theological Education.* Louisville: Westminster John Knox Press, 1995.

Collins, P. H. *Black Feminist Thought: Knowledge, Consciousness, and the Politics of Empowerment.* 2nd, rev. ed. New York: Routledge, 2000.

Coyle, J. M. *Handbook on Women and Aging.* Westport, Conn.: Greenwood Press, 1997.

Denizen, N. K., and Lincoln, Y. *Handbook of Qualitative Research.* Thousand Oaks, Calif.: Sage Publications, 1994.

Estes, C. *The Aging Enterprise.* San Francisco: Jossey-Bass, 1979.

_____. *Social Policy and Aging: A Critical Perspective.* Thousand Oaks, Calif.: Sage Publications, 2001.

Doyle, D. *Communion Ecclesiology.* Maryknoll, N.Y.: Orbis Books, 2000.

Fiddes, P. *Participating in God: A Pastoral Doctrine of the Trinity.* Louisville: Westminster John Knox Press, 2000.

Fischer, D. H. *Growing Old in America.* New York: Oxford University Press, 1977.

Freedman, J., and Combs, G. *Narrative Therapy: The Social Construction of Preferred Realities.* New York: W.W. Norton, 1996.

Gannon, L. *Women and Aging: Transcending the Myths: Women and Psychology.* London; New York: Routledge, 1999.

Gentzler, R., and Clingan, D. *Aging: God's Challenge to Church and Synagogue.* Nashville: Discipleship Resources, 1996.

Grenz, S. *The Social God and the Relational Self: A Trinitarian Theology of the Imago Dei.* Louisville: Westminster John Knox Press, 2001.

Harré, R. *The Singular Self: An Introduction to the Psychology of Personhood.* Thousand Oaks, Calif.: Sage Publications, 1998.

Hazan, H. *Old Age: Constructions and Deconstructions.* Cambridge: Cambridge University Press, 1994.

Hodgson, P. *Revisioning the Church: Ecclesial Freedom in the New Paradigm.* Minneapolis: Fortress Press, 1988.

Johnson, E. *Friends of God and Prophets: A Feminist Theological Reading of the Communion of Saints.* New York: Continuum, 1998.

Jones, S. *Feminist Theory and Christian Theology: Cartographies of Grace.* Minneapolis: Fortress Press, 2000.

Kimble, M. A., McFadden, S., Ellor J., and Seeber, J., eds. *Aging, Spirituality, and Religion.* Minneapolis: Fortress Press, 1995.

Koenig, H., and Weaver, A. *Counseling Troubled Older Adults.* Nashville: Abingdon Press, 1997.

Lacugna, C. *God for Us: The Trinity and Christian Life.* San Francisco: HarperCollins, 1991.

Lyon, K. B. *Toward a Practical Theology of Aging.* Theology and Pastoral Care Series. Philadelphia: Fortress Press, 1985.

Marshall, J. *Counseling Lesbian Women.* Louisville: Westminster John Knox Press, 1997.

McFadyen, A. I. *The Call to Personhood: A Christian Theory of the Individual in Social Relationships.* New York: Cambridge University Press, 1990.

Miller-McLemore, B., and Gill-Austern, B., eds. *Feminist and Womanist Pastoral Theology.* Nashville: Abingdon Press, 1999.

Mitchell, K., and Anderson H. *All Our Losses, All Our Griefs: Resources for Pastoral Care.* Philadelphia: Westminster Press, 1983.

Minkler, M., and Estes, C. *Critical Perspectives on Aging: The Political and Moral Economy of Growing Old.* Amityville, N.Y.: Baywood Publishing, 1991.

Schaie, K. W., and Hendricks, J. *The Evolution of the Aging Self: The Societal Impact on the Aging Process.* New York: Springer, 2000.

Stern, D. *The Interpersonal World of the Infant.* New York: Basic Books, 1985.

Thone, R. R. *Women and Aging: Celebrating Ourselves.* New York: Haworth Press, 1992.

Volf, M. *After Our Likeness: The Church as the Image of the Trinity.* Grand Rapids, Mich.: Eerdmans, 1998.

White, M., and Epston, D. *Narrative Means to Therapeutic Ends.* New York: W.W. Norton & Company, 1990.

Wimberly, A.S., ed. *Honoring African American Elders: A Ministry in the Soul Community.* San Francisco: Jossey-Bass, 1997.

Young, I.M. *Justice and the Politics of Difference.* Princeton, N.J.: Princeton University Press, 1990.

Notes

Chapter 1: Invisible Women

[1]U.S. Administration on Aging, *Profile of Older Americans, 2001* (Washington, D.C.: Center for Communication and Consumer Services, U.S. Department of Health and Human Services, 2001).

[2]Meredith Minkler and Carroll Estes, *Critical Perspectives on Aging: The Political and Moral Economy of Growing Old* (Amityville, N.Y.: Baywood Publishing, 1991), 3.

[3]See David Fischer, *Growing Older in America* (New York: Oxford Press, 1977), for a history of American attitudes toward aging.

[4]Ibid.

[5]See Ruth Thone, *Women and Aging: Celebrating Ourselves* (New York: Haworth, 1992); Jean Coyle, *Handbook on Women and Aging* (Westport, Conn.: Greenwood Press, 1997); and Sara Arber and Jay Ginn, *Gender and Late Life* (London: Sage, 1991) on invisibility. For further discussion of the social construction of aging see Jessie Alan and Alan Pifer, *Women on the Front Lines: A Sociological Analysis of Resources and Constraints*; Paul Thompson et al., *I Don't Feel Old: The Experience of Late Life* (New York: Oxford University Press, 1990); Linda Ganon, *Women and Aging: Transcending the Myths* (New York: Routledge, 1999); Carroll Estes, *The Aging Enterprise* (San Francisco: Jossey Bass, 1979); Carroll Estes, *Social Policy and Aging: A Critical Perspective* (Thousand Oaks, Calif.: Sage Publications, 2001).

[6]See Office of Research, General Council on Ministries, The United Methodist Church, *The 1994 Survey of United Methodist Opinion* (Dayton, Ohio), for more detailed church demographics.

[7]Bernice Neugarten, "Age Groups in American Society and the Rise of the Young-Old" in *Political Consequences of Aging*, ed. Frederick R. Eisele (Philadelphia: American Academy of Political and Social Sciences, 1974).

[8]*Meeting the Needs of Older Women*, U.S. Administration on Aging Fact Sheet, 2001 (Washington, D.C.: U.S. Administration on Aging, Department of Health and Human Service), available at www.aoainfor@aoa.gov.

[9]Ibid.

[10]Baba Copper, *Over the Hill: Reflections on Ageism Between Women* (Freedom, Calif.: Crossing Press, 1988).

[11]Carroll Estes, Karen Linkins, and Elizabeth Binney, "Critical Perspectives on Aging," in Estes, *Social Policy and Aging*, 25.

[12]See for example, K. Brynwolf Lyon, *Toward a Practical Theology of Aging* (Philadelphia: Fortress Press, 1985); Harold Koenig and Andrew Weaver, *Counseling Troubled Older Adults: A Handbook for Pastors and Religious Caregivers* (Nashville: Abingdon Press, 1997); Richard Gentzler and Donald Clingan, *God's Challenge to Church and Synagogue* (Nashville: Discipleship Resources, 1996).

[13]Because a significant study has focused on issues of women and poverty, I did not focus on this dimension. See Helene K. Black and Robert Rubenstein, *Old Souls: Aged Women, Poverty, and the Experience of God* (New York: Aldine De Gruyter, 2000).

[14]This portrait of the church reflects the perspective of communion ecclesiology. See Dennis Doyle, *Communion Ecclesiology* (Maryknoll, N.Y.: Orbis Books, 2000), for further description and discussion.

[15]See Bonnie Miller-McLemore and Brita Gill-Austern, *Feminist and Womanist Pastoral Theology* (Nashville: Abingdon Press, 1999), for a development of feminist pastoral theological method.

[16]See Rebecca Chopp, *Saving Work: Feminist Practices of Theological Education* (Louisville: Westminster John Knox Press, 1995), for a discussion of the critical

correlational method, an adaptation of David Tracy's revised correlational method developed in *Blessed Rage for Order* (New York: Seabury Press, 1975).

[17]My description of these levels of thinking is dependent on Don Browning's description of five levels of moral thinking as a refinement of the revised correlational method. See *A Fundamental Practical Theology: Descriptive Strategies and Proposals* (Minneapolis: Fortress Press, 1991).

[18]The resources I used to design my study were Norman K. Denzin and Yvonna S. Lincoln, eds., *Handbook of Qualitative Research* (Thousand Oaks, Calif.: Sage Publications, 1994); James P. Spradly, *The Ethnographic Interview* (Fort Worth, Tex.: Harcourt Brace Jovanovich, 1979); and Steinvar Kvale, *InterViews: An Introduction to Qualitative Research Interviewing* (Thousand Oaks, Calif.: Sage Publications, 1996).

[19]My use of metaphor reflects Don Browning's understanding of the visional level of moral thinking. See Browning, *A Fundamental Practical Theology*.

[20]Paul S. Fiddes, *Participating in God: A Pastoral Doctrine of the Trinity* (Louisville: Westminster John Knox Press, 2000).

[21]K. Brynolf Lyon, *Toward a Practical Theology of Aging* (Philadelphia: Fortress Press, 1985).

[22]Alistair McFayden, *The Call To Personhood: A Christian Theory of the Individual in Social Relationships* (New York: Cambridge University Press, 1990).

[23]See Lyon, *Toward a Practical Theology of Aging*.

[24]Miroslav Volf, *After Our Likeness: The Church as the Image of the Trinity* (Grand Rapids, Mich.: Eerdmans, 1998). Elizabeth Johnson, *Friends of God and Prophets: A Feminist Theological Reading of the Communion of Saints* (New York: Continuum, 1998).

[25]See Victor Marshall, "The State of Theory in Aging in the Social Sciences" in *Handbook of Aging in the Social Sciences,* 4th ed., ed. Robert Binstock and Linda K. George (New York: Academic Press, 1996) pp. 12–30.

[26]Both disengagement theory and activity theory, which followed it, sought to provide generalized explanations for behavior in old age and are examples of normative theories, ibid., 20.

[27]Ibid., 14.

[28]Some of the theorists working within this critical perspective who inform my work include Estes, Arber and Ginn, and Robert Atchley (see note 30). See also Marshall, in Binstock and George, *Handbook of Aging,* 23; Estes, *Social Policy and Aging;* and Minkler and Estes, *Critical Perspectives on Aging.*

[29]Estes, *The Aging Enterprise* and *Social Policy and Aging.*

[30]Robert Atchley, *Continuity and Adaptation in Aging: Creating Positive Experiences* (Baltimore: Johns Hopkins University Press, 1999).

[31]By old-line Protestant denominations I mean those that have also been refered to as mainline, are primarily European American in membership composition, and usually include Methodists, Presbyterians, Lutherans, Episcopalians, and some Baptists. Many of these denominations are experiencing declines in membership and aging congregations.

[32]For an excellent study on aging in the African American church, see Ann Streaty Wimberly, ed., *Honoring African American Elders: A Ministry in the Soul Community* (San Francisco: Jossey Bass, 1997).

[33]Although fifteen women were interviewed, I have used excerpts from only eleven of these because of technical difficulties with the remaining four, such as recording problems, or the quality of the interviews.

[34]This study was conducted by fifteen of my students at Saint Paul School of Theology in Kansas City, Mo., for a course titled "Pastoral Care of Women." I have used material only from women who signed a consent form permitting my use of the interviews.

Chapter 2: The Cultural Construction of Old Age

[1]K. J. Gergen and Mary M. Gergen, "The New Aging: Self Construction and Social Values," in *Social Structures and Aging,* ed. K.W. Schaie (New York: Springer,

2000). Gergen and Gergen's analysis focuses on the personal levels of meaning construction and operates primarily at the microtheoretical level.

[2]I am using Carroll Estes's political economy theory on aging to examine how social forces, such as market and economic factors like the state, together with public policy shape the meanings of aging. Her theory can be considered a macro-level constructivist theory.

[3]Mary M. Gergen and Sara N. Davis, *Toward a New Psychology of Gender* (New York: Routledge Press, 1997), 5.

[4]Haim Hazan, *Old Age: Constructions and Deconstructions* (Cambridge, U.K.: Cambridge University Press, 1994), 13.

[5]See ibid., 13–32.

[6]Ibid., 16.

[7]Iris Marion Young, *Justice and the Politics of Difference* (Princeton, N.J.: Princeton University Press, 1990), 59.

[8]Ibid.

[9]Ibid.

[10]Ibid.

[11]Ibid., 62. See also pages 132–35.

[12]Ibid., 59.

[13]Ibid, 98–99.

[14]Patricia Hill Collins, *Black Feminist Thought,* 2d ed. (New York: Routledge, 2002), 68.

[15]Ibid., 60.

[16]Lois Banner, *In Full Flower: Aging Women, Power and Sexuality* (New York: Knopf, 1992), 190.

[17]Elizabeth Markson, " Sagacious, Sinful, or Superfluous? The Social Construction of Older Women," in *Handbook on Women and Aging,* ed. Jean M. Coyle (Westport, Conn.: Greenwood Press, 1997), 57.

[18]Ibid., 59.

[19]Heinrich Kramer and Jacob Sprenger, *Malleus Maleficarum,* trans. Montague Summers (New York: Dover, 1971), 49, cited in Banner, *In Full Flower,* 191.

[20]Banner, *In Full Flower,* 190.

[21]Markson, "Sagacious," 57.

[22]Ibid., 58.

[23]Ibid.

[24]Ibid.

[25]Older women, African Americans, and the poor elderly were not venerated. David Fischer, *Growing Old in America* (New York: Oxford University Press, 1977).

[26]Carole Haber, "Witches, Widows, Wives, and Workers: The Historiography of Elderly Women in America," in Coyle, *Handbook.*

[27]Ibid., 30.

[28]Ibid., 31.

[29]Ibid.

[30]Ibid.

[31]Thomas Cole, *The Journey of Life: The History of Aging in America* (Cambridge, UK.: Cambridge University Press, 1992), 161–62.

[32]Ibid.

[33]Ibid., xxv.

[34]Ibid., xxiv.

[35]Ibid.

[36]Ibid., 91.

[37]Ibid.

[38]Markson, "Sagacious," 60. See also Carole Haber, *Beyond Sixty-five: The Dilemma of Old Age in America's Past* (New York: Cambridge University Press, 1983).

[39]Markson, "Sagacious," 58.

[40]The first instance of this appeared in New York's constitution in 1777. Fischer, *Growing Old in America,* 80.

[41]Carroll Estes and Elizabeth Binney, "The Biomedicalization of Aging: Dangers and Dilemmas," in *Critical Perspectives on Aging: The Political and Moral Economy of Growing Old,* ed. Meredith Minkler and Carroll Estes (Amityville, N.Y.: Baywood Publishing, 1991), 117.

[42]Hazan, *Old Age,* 15.

[43]Ibid.

[44]See Tom Koch, *Age Speaks for Itself: Silent Voices of the Elderly* (Westport, Conn.: Praeger, 2000), for a further discussion of this image of the aged.

[45]Hazan, *Old Age,* 14. See also Banner, *In Full Flower,* for a fuller discussion of the association of the witch with older women.

[46]Hazan, *Old Age,* 28.

[47]Beth Warren, "Senior Encouragement Project Helps Energize Elderly," *Atlanta Journal Constitution,* 8 November 2002.

[48]Young, *Justice and the Politics of Difference,* 129. This applied only to white women. Black women were also defined as physically deviant, but the cultural construction of their bodies was different from that of white women. Patricia Hill Collins, in *Black Feminist Thought,* has addressed this in her images of mammy and Jezebel. One was a sexualized image, whereas the other was asexual and existed for the nurture of others. Both white and black women become particularly identified with sexuality, but in different ways.

[49]Ibid.

[50]Ibid., 129–30.

[51]Carrrol Estes, Steven P. Wallace, Karen Linkins, and Elizabeth Binney, "The Medicalization and Commodification of Aging and the Privatization and Rationalization of Old Age Policy," in *Social Policy and Aging: A Critical Perspective,* ed. Carroll Estes (Thousand Oaks, Calif.: Sage Publications, 2001), 46.

[52]Ibid.

[53]Lisa Davis, "New Cures, New Fears," *Reader's Digest,* October 2002.

[54]Estes and Binney, "Biomedicalization," 128–29.

[55]Estes et al., "Medicalization and Commodification,"46.

[56]Ibid.

[57]Ibid.

[58]Chiquita Collins, Carroll Estes, and Julia Bradsher, "Inequality in Aging: The Creation of Dependency," in Estes, *Social Policy and Aging: A Critical Perspective,* 138.

[59]Hazan, *Old Age,* 5.

[60]Ibid., 21.

[61]Jack Ziegler, *The New Yorker,* 22 April, 2002, 206. This view is also represented in some academic publications. For example, in Gerkin's chapter on aging, the paradigm of aging as loss is quite evident. See Charles Gerkin, *Introduction to Pastoral Care* (Nashville: Abingdon Press, 1997).

[62]Koch, *Age Speaks,* 2.

[63]Ibid., 3.

[64]Ibid., 1.

[65]Glenda Laws, "Understanding Ageism: Lessons from Feminism and Postmodernism" *The Gerontologist* 35, no. 1 (1995): 112–18.

[66]Mary Lee Hummert, "Physiognomic Cues to Age and the Activation of Stereotypes of the Elderly in Interaction," *International Journal of Aging and Human Development* 39, no. 1 (1994): 5–19.

[67]Ibid.

[68]Young, *Justice and the Politics of Difference,* 123.

[69]Ibid., 123–24.

[70]Nancy Signorielli, "Aging on Television: The Picture in the Nineties," *Generations* 25, no. 3 (Fall 2001): 34–38.

[71]Markson, "Sagacious," 65.

[72]Ibid., 66.

[73]Ibid.

[74]Susan Sherman, "Images of Middle-aged and Older Women: Historical, Cultural, and Personal," in Coyle, *Handbook,* 17; Marilyn Maxwell, "Portraits of Menopausal Women in Selected Works of English and American Literature," in *The Meanings of Menopause: Historical, Medical, and Clinical Perspectives,* ed. Ruth Fromanek (Hillsdale, N.J.: Analytic Press, 1990), 255–80.

[75]Judith de Luce, "Silence at the Newsstand," *Generations* 25, no. 3 (Fall 2001): 39–43.

[76]These results emerged from interviews with fifteen older widows conducted by my students in the course Pastoral Care of Women in Fall 1997. The students kept written records of the interviews and obtained consent for participation in the project. The names of the participants have been changed in accordance with the consent agreement. The women in this study resided in a rural part of the Midwest. Twelve of the fifteen were white, three were African American; most of the women were working class and not college educated.

[77]Patricia Miller, Darryl Miller, Eithne McKibbin, and Gregory Pettys, "Stereotypes of Elderly in Magazine Advertisements 1956–1996," *International Journal of Aging and Human Development* 49, no. 4 (1999): 319–37.

[78]See Banner, *In Full Flower,* for a fuller discussion of the historical development of these images.

[79]Hummert, "Physiognomic Cues," 8.

[80]Miller et al., "Stereotypes of Elderly," 321.

[81]Ibid., 323–24.

[82]Collins, *Black Feminist Thought,* 73.

[83]Ibid., 81.

[84]Ibid., 81–83.

[85]Ibid.

[86]Collins, *Black Feminist Thought,* 68.

[87]Cole, *Journey of Life,* 33.

[88]Ibid., 233.

[89]Ibid.

[90]See, for example, Eugene Bianchi, *Aging as a Spiritual Journey* (New York: Crossroads, 1982). See also Melvin Kimble et al., eds., *Aging, Spirituality and Religion: A Handbook* (Minneapolis: Fortress Press, 1995), and David Moberg, ed., *Aging and Spirituality: Spiritual Dimensions of Aging Theory, Research, Procedure, and Policy* (New York: Haworth Pastoral Press, 2001.)

Chapter 3: Challenging Invisibility

[1]These vignettes are constructions based on the experiences of the women interviewed for this project, with some details changed to protect anonymity. Some are composites, representing features of stories from two or more of the women interviewed. I am using *church* in a broad sense here to mean the Christian church as a whole. Particular communities of faith will be referred to as *congregations* or *communities of faith.*

[2]I am relying primarily here on the anthropology of Alistair McFayden articulated in *The Call to Personhood: A Christian Theory of the Individual in Social Relationships* (Cambridge, U.K.: Cambridge University Press, 1990). For a further discussion of a Trinitarian anthropology, see Stanley Grenz, *The Social God and the Relational Self: A Trinitarian Theology of the Imago Dei* (Louisville: Westminster John Knox Press, 2001); Paul S. Fiddes, *Participating in God: A Pastoral Doctrine of the Trinity* (Louisville: Westminster John Knox Press, 2001); and Catherine Mowry LaCugna, *God for Us: The Trinity and Christian Life* (San Francisco: HarperCollins, 1991).

[3]See LaCugna, *God for Us,* and Grenz, *The Social God,* for a discussion of the developments in Trinitarian theology informing this anthropology.

⁴Miroslav Volf, *After Our Likeness: The Church as the Image of the Trinity* (Grand Rapids, Mich.: Eerdmans, 1998), 182–83.

⁵LaCugna, *God for Us,* 256. LaCugna is citing John MacMurray's work here as informing her understanding of personhood.

⁶Volf, *After Our Likeness,* 183.

⁷K. Brynolf Lyon, *Toward a Practical Theology of Aging* (Philadelphia: Fortress Press, 1985).

⁸Ibid., 91.

⁹Ibid., 47.

¹⁰Ibid., 103.

¹¹Ibid., 104.

¹²*Church* as used here usually means primarily the Protestant and Roman Catholic Churches, predominantly European American. See Robert Bellah et al., *Habits of the Heart: Individualism and Commitment in American Life* (New York: Harper and Row, 1986), for an analysis of the increasing individualism of American culture.

¹³Rebecca Chopp, *Saving Work: Feminist Practices of Theological Education* (Louisville: Westminster John Knox Press, 1995), 45.

¹⁴Peter Hodgson, *Revisioning the Church: Ecclesial Freedom in the New Paradigm* (Minneapolis: Fortress Press, 1988), 64.

¹⁵"The conservatives have lost relevance, the liberals have lost transcendence; hence both have capitulated to the demands of the culture and can readily subserve political, social, and economic interests" (Hodgson, 64). For a further development of this argument see Hodgson, *Revisioning the Church.*

¹⁶Peter Hodgson and Robert C. Williams, "The Church," in *Christian Theology and an Introduction to Its Traditions and Tasks,* ed. Peter Hodgson and Robert King (Minneapolis: Fortress Press, 1994), 249–73.

¹⁷Ibid.

¹⁸Ibid.

¹⁹See Don Browning, *A Fundamental Practical Theology: Descriptive Strategies and Proposals* (Minneapolis: Fortress Press, 1991) for a further discussion of this claim.

²⁰Dennis Doyle, *Communion Ecclesiology* (Maryknoll, N.Y.: Orbis Books, 2000), 2. See also Thomas Best and Gunther Gassman, *On the Way to Fuller Koinonia: Faith and Order Paper No. 166* (Geneva: WCC Publications, 1994).

²¹This vision of church is inspired by Mirslav Volf's vision of church in *After Our Likeness* and his concept of embrace in *Exclusion and Embrace: A Theological Exploration of Identity, Otherness and Reconciliation* (Nashville: Abingdon Press, 1996). The concept of circle also finds resonance in Letty Russell's concept of the church in the round, *Church in the Round: Feminist Interpretation of the Church* (Louisville: Westminster John Knox Press, 1993). This particular development, however, is my own.

²²For of a full exposition of various approaches of communion ecclesiology, see, for example, Best and Gassman, *On the Way to Fuller Koinonia;* Jean-Marie Tillard, *Church of Churches: The Ecclesiology of Communion* (Collegeville: The Liturgical Press, 1987); Volf, *After Our Likeness;* Jean Zizioulas, *Being as Communion: Studies in Personhood and the Church* (Crestwood, N.Y.: St. Vladimir's Seminary Press, 1985); Elizabeth Johnson, *Friends of God and Prophets: A Feminist Theological Reading of the Communion of Saints* (New York: Continuum Publishing, 1998).

²³Doyle, *Communion Ecclesiology,* 13.

²⁴Ibid.

²⁵Ibid., 12.

²⁶Ibid., 14.

²⁷Ibid.

²⁸Ibid.

²⁹Ibid., 15.

³⁰There are various ways and means through which this vision becomes embodied. Here I focus on how this vision of church impacts older women and the expression of this vision through practices of care. This vision hopefully addresses

other marginalized groups as well and could be expressed through other practices of ministry.

[31]This model of care seeks to both integrate features of the classical, clinical, and communal-contextual models of care as well as move beyond these models.

[32]Chopp, *Saving Work,* 15.

[33]Dorothy Bass and Craig Dykstra, "A Theological Understanding of Christian Practices," in *Practicing Theology: Beliefs and Practices in Christian Life,* ed. Miroslav Volf and Dorothy Bass (Grand Rapids, Mich.: Eerdmans, 2002), 6–8.

[34]Phillip Culbertson, *Caring for God's People: Counseling and Christian Wholeness* (Minneapolis: Fortress Press, 2000).

[35]I borrow this term from Rebecca Chopp, who uses it in a somewhat different context in *Saving Work,* 21.

[36]For a further discussion of hospitality, see Anna Maria Pineda, "Hospitality," in *Practicing Our Faith,* ed. Dorothy C. Bass (San Francisco: Jossey Bass, 1997). See also Thomas Ogletree, *Hospitality to the Stranger: Dimensions of Moral Understanding* (Philadelphia: Fortress Press, 1985).

[37]Personal conversation with Richard Gentzler, director of the United Methodist Center on Aging and Older Adult Ministries, September 2002. These observations were based on preliminary reports of a survey of the most common forms of older adult ministry in United Methodist congregations.

Chapter 4: Narrative Practices of Care

[1]Donald E. Polkinghorne, *Narrative Knowing and the Human Sciences* (Albany, N.Y.: SUNY Press, 1988).

[2]Ibid.

[3]Ibid., 5.

[4]Although significant decreases in income status and poor health status are two factors that can significantly impact one's sense of well-being following retirement, these factors are not present in these cases. None of three women in the following case studies faced significant loss of income as a consequence of retirement. Although two of the women had some health limitations, these were not disabling in either case.

[5]Herbert Anderson and Edward Foley, *Mighty Stories, Dangerous Rituals: Weaving Together the Human and Divine* (San Francisco: Jossey-Bass, 1998), 5.

[6]Gubrium and Holstein, *New Language,* 147.

[7]Anderson and Foley, *Mighty Stories,* xiii.

[8]I am combining elements of both Daniel Stern and Rom Harré's various dimensions of self. Although it might be argued that these senses of self are not compatible, I am combining them for heuristic purposes here in order to discuss various dimensions of narrative.

[9]My own understanding of personality theory is informed by the work of Daniel Stern, *The Interpersonal World of the Infant* (New York: Basic Books, 1985), and Rom Harré, *The Singular Self: An Introduction to the Psychology of Personhood* (Thousand Oaks, Calif.: Sage, 1998). Stern argues that we have a sense of self from birth, but this sense of self is essentially formed in a relational matrix. I am influenced by Stern's personality theory for the ideas presented in this section. My discussion here is informed by Stern's concepts of the four senses of self—emergent, core, subjective, and verbal—and the four domains of relatedness that cohere into personal identity. Drawing on Harré's work, I assume that although persons exist, the self is not an entity, but a description used to capture our experience of singularity and identity. Harré identifies three senses of self that comprise our experience of personhood: one's point of view, from which one perceives ands acts upon the world (self 1); a collection of attributes that distinguish one as a unique person (self 2); and the impression one has of others and the perceptions others have of that person (self 3) (Harré, 4). A point on which Harré and Stern differ is that Harré assumes that although persons exist, the self is not an entity but a description used to capture our experience of singularity and identity.

[10]See Daniel Stern's discussion of the subjective sense of self and the domain of intersubjective relatedness. His concepts inform my discussion here.

[11]This description is of an actual church community. The name has been changed here.

[12]Andrew Lester, *Hope in Pastoral Care and Counseling* (Louisville: Westminster John Knox Press, 1995).

[13]Ibid.

[14]I will draw particularly on the work of Michael White and David Epston, *Narrative Means to Therapeutic Ends* (New York: W.W. Norton, 1990). See also Jill Freedman and Gene Combs, *Narrative Therapy: The Social Construction of Preferred Realities* (New York: W.W. Norton, 1996); and Gerald Monk, John Winslade, Kathie Crocket, and David Epston, eds., *Narrative Therapy in Practice: The Archaeology of Hope* (San Francisco: Jossey-Bass, 1997).

[15]White and Epston, *Narrative Means,* 3.

[16]Ibid., 3–4.

[17]Ibid., 15.

[18]Robert Atchley, *Continuity and Adaptation in Aging: Creating Positive Experiences* (Baltimore: Johns Hopkins University Press, 1999), vii.

[19]Ibid., 3.

[20]Ibid., 1.

[21]Ibid., 2.

[22]Ibid., 6.

Chapter 5: Tending Relationships–Single Women in Later Life

[1]This claim reflects the relational anthropology articulated in chapter 2. It also reflects Daniel Stern's theory of development and narrative therapy theory, both detailed in chapter 3. Narrative therapy theory arises out of family systems theory, which asserts that personality and behavior are formed by the relational systems in which we participate. For a further discussion of systems theory, see, for example, Edwin Freidman, *From Generation to Generation: Family Process in Church and Synagogue* (New York: Guilford Press, 1985).

[2]Richard Newtson and Pat M. Keith, "Single Women in Later Life," in *Handbook on Women and Aging,* ed. Jean Coyle (Westport, Conn.: Greenwood Press, 1997), 387.

[3]Toni C. Antonucci, in *Women Growing Older: Psychological Perspectives,* ed. Barbara Turner and Lillian Troll (Thousand Oaks, Calif.: Sage Publications, 1994), 239–69. See also Linda Gannon, *Women and Aging: Transcending the Myths* (New York: Routledge, 1999).

[4]Catherine Keller, *From a Broken Web: Separation, Sexism, and Self* (Boston: Beacon Press, 1986). See also Bonnie Miller McLemore, "The Living Human Web," in *Through the Eyes of Women: Insights for Pastoral Care,* ed. Jean Moessner (Minneapolis: Fortress Press, 1996).

[5]See Serene Jones, *Feminist Theory and Christian Theology: Cartographies of Grace* (Minneapolis: Fortress Press, 2000), for a discussion of the essentialist and social constructivist debate in feminist thought.

[6]U.S. Administration on Aging, *Profile of Older Americans, 2001* (Washington, D.C.: Center for Communication and Consumer Services, U.S. Department of Health and Human Services, 2001).

[7]Newtson and Keith, "Single Women in Later Life."

[8]Ibid., 386.

[9]I have known Kate for some time as a personal friend. I often discussed this project on older women with Kate and her mother on visits before I began the formal interviews. Although I did not use the formal interview protocol with Kate that I used with later participants, with her permission I recorded her answers to my informal questions. These informal conversations helped me determine the interview protocol

and shaped the project in a number of ways. Kate and her mother's name have both been changed.

[10]Newtson and Keith, "Single Women in Later Life," 387.

[11]Ibid.

[12]Ibid.

[13]Ibid.

[14]Ibid.

[15]Victor Cicirelli, *Helping Elderly Parents: The Role of Adult Children* (Boston: Auburn House, 1981), cited in ibid., 389.

[16]Timothy Brubaker, *Later Life in Families* (Newbury Park, Calif.: Sage, 1985), cited in ibid.

[17]Newston and Keith, "Single Women in Later Life," 390.

[18]Ibid.

[19]U.S. Census Bureau, United States Department of Commerce, "Current Population Survey," *The Older Population in the United States: March 2000* (Washington D.C.: U.S. Govt.), Detailed Tables (PPL-147), available at http://www.census.gov/population/www/socdemo/age/ppl-147.html.

[20]Helena Z. Lopata, *Widowhood in an American City* (Cambridge, Mass.: Schenkman, 1973); *Women as Widows* (New York: Elsevier, 1979); *Current Widowhood: Myths and Realities* (Thousand Oaks, Calif.: Sage, 1996).

[21]U.S. Census Bureau, United States Department of Commerce, "Current Population Survey," *The Older Population in the United States: March 2000* (Washington D.C.: U.S. Govt.), Detailed Tables (PPL-147), available at http://www.census.gov/population/www/socdemo/age/ppl-147.html.

[22]Dale Lund, Michael Casserta, and Margaret Diamond, "Impact of Spousal Bereavement on the Subjective Well Being of Older Adults," in *Older Bereaved Spouses*, ed. Dale A.. Lund (New York: Hemisphere Publishing, 1989).

[23]Helena Z. Lopata *Current Widowhood,* 107.

[24]Lopata, *Widowhood in an American City.*

[25]Anabel Pelham and William Clark, "Widowhood Among Low Income Racial and Ethnic Groups in California," in *Widows,* vol. 2, *North America,* ed. Helena Lopata (Durham, N.C.: Duke Univ. Press 1987), 191–224.

[26]Joan's experience is reflected in a study by Kathleen A. Glass, "Appraisal, Coping and Resources: Markers Associated with the Health of Aged Widows and Widowers," in Lund, *Older Bereaved Spouses.* This study of urban women associated with Catholic parishes found that church attendance and religious beliefs were helpful in adjusting to the husband's death.

[27]See Jeffery S. Levin and Sheldon Tobin, "Religion and Psychological Well-Being," in *Aging, Spirituality, and Religion: A Handbook,* ed. Melvin Kimble, Susan McFadden, James Ellor, and James Seeber (Minneapolis: Fortress Press, 1995).

[28]Ibid.

[29]Tonya Schuster and Edgar W. Butler, "Bereavement, Social Networks, Social Support, and Mental Health,"in Lund, *Older Bereaved Spouses.* See also Julia E. Bradsher, "Older Women and Widowhood," in Coyle, *Handbook,* 426.

[30]Lopata, *Widowhood,* 43.

[31]A widow is usually defined as a married woman whose husband has died. I am expanding the term here to include the loss of nonmarried life partners, either of the same sex or opposite sex.

[32]For a more detailed discussion on pastoral care with widows, see Karen Scheib, "Older Widows: Surviving, Thriving, and Reinventing One's Life," in *In Her Own Time: Women and Developmental Issues in Pastoral Care,* ed. Jean Moessner (Minneapolis: Fortress Press, 2000).

[33]For more detailed pastoral strategies in responding to particular stages of grief, see Kenneth Mitchell and Herbert Anderson, *All Our Losses, All Our Griefs: Resources for Pastoral Care* (Philadelphia: Westminster Press, 1983).

[34]For more detail on complications of bereavement, see Rosalyn Karaban, *Complicated Losses, Difficult Deaths: A Practical Guide for Ministering to Grievers* (San Jose, Calif.: Resource Publications, 2000). See also Therese Rando, *Treatment of Complicated Mourning* (Champaign, Ill.: Research Press, 1993).

[35]Phyllis R. Silverman, *Widow-to-Widow* (New York: Springer, 1986).

[36]Schuster and Butler, "Bereavement."

[37]The Shepherd's Center Program began in Kansas City, Missouri, in partnership with area churches. It is now nationwide and provides a variety of programs, mostly educational for older adults by older adults. For more information, go to www.shepherdcenters.org.

[38]Jean Pearson Scott, "Family Relationships of Midlife and Older Women," in Coyle, *Handbook,* 374.

[39]Nancy Hooyman and H. Asuman Kiyak, *Social Gerontology* (Needham Heights, Mass.: Allyn and Bacon, 1992), cited in Scott, "Family Relationships."

[40]Scott, 374.

[41]C.L. Hayes and D. Anderson, "Psycho-Social and Economic Adjustment of Mid-Life Women after Divorce: A National Study," *Journal of Women and Aging* 4 (1993):83–99, cited in Coyle, *Handbook,* 375.

[42]Scott, 375.

[43]Ibid.

Chapter 6: Tending Relationships–
Marriage, Partnership, Family, and Friends

[1]Jean Pearson Scott, "Family Relationships of Midlife and Older Women," in *Handbook on Women and Aging,* ed. Jean Coyle (Westport, Conn.: Greenwood Press, 1997), 376.

[2]See Dorothy Jerome, "Intimacy and Sexuality Amongst Older Women," in *Women Come of Age,* ed. Miriam Bernard and Kathy Meade (London: Edward Arnold, 1993).

[3]James Nelson and Sandra P. Longfellow, eds., "Introduction," in *Sexuality and the Sacred: Sources for Theological Reflection* (Louisville: Westminster John Knox Press, 1994), xiv.

[4]See, for example, *Over the Hill: Reflections on Ageism Between Women* (Freedom, Calif.: Crossing Press, 1988); see also Barbara McDonald with Cynthia Rich, *Look Me in the Eye: Old Women, Aging, and Ageism* (San Francisco: Spinsters/Aunt Lute, 1983).

[5]Ibid.

[6]My thanks to Anne Carey for her insights informing my thoughts in this section. Personal correspondence, 12 January 2003.

[7]Joretta Marshall, *Counseling Lesbian Women* (Louisville: Westminster John Knox Press, 1997).

[8]Jerome, "Intimacy and Sexuality," 103.

[9]Kenneth Doka, *Disenfranchised Loss: Recognizing Hidden Sorrow* (Lexington, Mass.: Lexington Books, 1989).

[10]Ibid.

[11]Scott, "Family Relationships," 370. Results from a study by Lauer, Lauer, and Kerr of one hundred couples married for forty-five years or more.

[12]Adapted from Robert Beavers, *Successful Marriage: A Family Systems Approach to Couples Therapy* (New York: W.W. Norton, 1985).

[13]Pauline Sutcliffe, Guinevere Tufnell, and Ursula Cornish, *Working with the Dying and Bereaved* (New York: Routledge, 1998), xiii.

[14]Herbert Anderson, "Family, Pastoral Care and Counseling of," in *Dictionary of Pastoral Care and Counseling,* ed. Rodney Hunter (Nashville: Abingdon Press, 1990).

[15]Linda Ade-Ridder, "Sexuality and Marital Quality Among Older Married Couples," in *Family Relationships in Later Life,* ed. Timothy Brubaker (Newbury Park: Sage Publications, 1990).

[16]Scott, "Family Relationships," 370.

[17]Jerome, "Intimacy and Sexuality," 87.

[18]Rebecca Adams, "Friendship Patterns Among Older Women," in Coyle, *Handbook.*

[19]Ibid., 410.

Chapter 7: Prophetic Practices of Care

[1]Chiquita Collins, Carroll L. Estes, and Julia Bradsher, "Inequality in Aging: The Creation of Dependency," in *Social Policy and Aging: A Critical Perspective,* ed. Carroll L. Estes (Thousand Oaks, Calif.: Sage Publications, 2001), 149.

[2]Economic security, access to health care and caregiving, and freedom from abuse are issues that have been identified by organizations such as the Older Women's League and the American Association of Retired Persons as concerns requiring advocacy on behalf of older women.

[3]U.S. Administration on Aging, *Profile of Older Americans, 2001,* Center for Communication and Consumer Services, U.S. Department of Health and Human Services, Washington, D.C.

[4]U.S. Administration on Aging, *Needs of Older Women, 2000,* Center for Communication and Consumer Services, U.S. Department of Health and Human Services, Washington, D.C.

[5]Ibid.

[6]Helen K. Black and Robert L. Rubinstein, *Old Souls: Aged Women, Poverty, and the Experience of God* (New York: Aldine De Gruyter, 2000), 11.

[7]Ibid., 12–13.

[8]Information from all these organizations and others is available via the Internet. The Women's Institute for a Secure Retirement and the National Center on Women and Aging nonprofit educational and advocacy groups both have educational resources available on financial planning for older women. Information regarding SSI, Medicaid, and food stamps is available from the Social Security Administration. AARP also has information about these programs at its Web site.

[9]Rose Rubin, "The Economic Status of Older Women," in Jean Coyle, ed., *Handbook on Women and Aging* (Westport, Conn.: Greenwood Press, 1997), 89.

[10]Ibid.

[11]Ibid.

[12]Carol Adams, *Woman-Battering* (Minneapolis: Fortress Press, 1994), 12.

[13]Ibid., 13.

[14]Ibid.

[15]National Committee for the Prevention of Elder Abuse Web site, www.preventelderabuse.org.

[16]Harold Koenig and Andrew Weaver, *Counseling Troubled Older Adults* (Nashville: Abingdon Press, 1997).

[17]Ibid.

[18]Ibid, 218–19.

[19]Kathleen Quinn, *Older Women: Hidden Sexual Abuse Victims,* U.S. Department on Aging, www.aoa.gov.

[20]For a further exploration of the biblical and theological foundations for opposing violence against women, see Carol Adams and Marie Fortune, *Violence Against Women and Children: A Christian Theological Sourcebook* (New York: Continuum, 1995).

[21]Don O'Briant, "Making it to 100," *Atlanta-Journal Constitution,* 15 January 2003.

[22]U.S. Administration on Aging, "Family Caregiving Fact Sheet," U.S. Center for Communication and Consumer Services, U.S. Department of Health and Human Services (Washington D.C., May 2001).

[23]National Alliance for Caregiving and American Association of Retired Persons Family Caregiving in the U.S., *Findings from a National Survey, Final Report* (Bethesda, Md.: National Alliance for Caregiving; Washingtion, D.C.: American Association of Retired Persons, 1997), available at www.caregiversmarketplace.com/Articles.

[24]Ibid.

[25]Phyllis Moen, Julie Robinson, and Vivian Fields, "Women's Work and Caregiving Roles," *Journal of Gerontology: Social Sciences* 49, no. 4, 1994.

[26]Barbara Payne-Stancil, "Religion and Faith Development of Older Women," in Coyle, *Handbook,* 232.

[27]U.S. Administration on Aging, "Family Caregiving Fact Sheet."

[28]Barbara Payne-Stancil, "Religion and Faith Development of Older Women," in Coyle, *Handbook,* 232.

[29]National Family Caregivers Association, "A Profile of Caregivers."

Index of Subjects

Index of Names and Authors